READY ENOUGH

Your 7-Step Guide for Life's Hardest Decisions

Marin Laukka

Disclaimer: All stories and examples provided throughout this book are shared with permission. To maintain the anonymity of the individuals involved, some details within the stories and examples, including involved persons' names, have been changed. Coaching and the contents of this book are not to be used as a substitute for professional advice by legal, mental, medical, financial, or other qualified professionals.

ISBN: 978-1-7374480-1-3 (Paperback)
ISBN: 978-1-7374480-4-4 (Audiobook)
ISBN: 978-1-7374480-0-6 (eBook)
ISBN: 978-1-7374480-2-0 (Hardcover)

Author: Marin Laukka, MA
Editors: Amy Pattee Colvin and Melinda Campbell
Cover Design: Damonza.com
Illustrator: Gunjan
Formatting: FormattedBooks.com
Author Photograph: Elyse Rethlake
Writing Coach: Jennifer Locke

https://www.yesandbymarin.com

Before You Begin…
Claim Your Free Workbook!

To get the most out of your reading experience and enact transformation within your own life, **download your free Alignment Journey Workbook** —including additional practices for each stage of your Alignment Journey.

**Visit yesandbymarin.com/workbook
to receive yours today,
or scan the QR code below:**

CONTENTS

Chapter 1   Lost in the River: Set Your Scene 1

Chapter 2   Find Your Compass: Who Are You
             Listening To? 16

Chapter 3   Float to the Riverbank: Create Space for
             Transformation 29

Chapter 4   Observe Your Surroundings: Clarify
             Your Truth 46

Chapter 5   Set Your Direction: Admit Your Desire 63

Chapter 6   Start Walking: Take Aligned Action 82

Chapter 7   Embrace Your Switchbacks: Trust
             the Ride 102

Chapter 8   Enjoy the View: Celebrate Your
             Alignment 122

Chapter 9   Discover More: Begin Again 138

Chapter 10   Ready Enough: You Are Not Alone 165

The Alignment Journey Stages

 Create Space for Transformation

 Clarify Your Truth

 Admit Your Desire

 Take Aligned Action

 Trust the Ride

 Celebrate Your Alignment

 Begin Again

DEDICATION

To my parents, Ginny and Mark Laukka,
for your relentless patience, love, and support.

CHAPTER 1

Lost in the River: Set Your Scene

Every now and then, I see a light escape your tightly sealed container.

A beam shoots from your core and dances across the ceiling. It excites anyone who stands around you and illuminates parts of the world I would not have otherwise seen. Your passion and excitement are contagious; it is as if your far-off dream is right in front of us.

But as many times as you speak to this dream, you also squander it with simple phrases, such as "maybe in my next life."

How easy it is to extinguish your dream with one sentence.

I watch as you mold yourself into the shape someone else created for you. You erase the scribbles you had excitedly colored outside of the lines. You cast aside your courageous vision as unrealistic, too much, or not enough.

My heart breaks when I hear you dismiss your quiet, daring voice. Yet, as you curve the edges of your lips into a "life is fine" smile to justify what is less than your true self and greatest alignment, I feel empathy, as well.

Your current reality is known. Up until this moment, you questioned: What could be wrong with what is safe and comfortable, that which is right as defined by those around me?

Today, I empower you to ask: Is known worth feeling disappointed, without purpose, and resentful as I choose to diminish my light, time and time again? Is this reality safe, comfortable, and right for me? Or am I simply afraid of wanting more?

I Do Not Know What Is Best for You

Let me start by clarifying what I do not know: I do not know what is best for you. This is something my first mentor, Coby Kozlowski, introduced during my life coach certification years ago. To this day, I hold this truth as a center point throughout my work as a coach, speaker, and author.

I do not claim to have your answers, and I never will.

This manuscript is not another rulebook for you to mindlessly adopt. These activities are not lists to check off for a sense of accomplishment without real, authentic change. Rather, this book is for those who are ready to admit that always seeking outside of yourself has led to more confusion and disappointment than fulfillment and success. This is for the beautiful humans who have done it all "right," yet lack the peaceful, confident, and content life to show for it.

Ultimately, I believe there is no greater wisdom than your own. I do not have your solution because I am not trying to fix you. You are not broken, you are curious. You are ready to pause the external seeking and step, more fully, into your authentic life.

As your coach and guide along this journey, I aid in the illumination of values, ambitions, and action steps you already know—even if you cannot yet articulate or see them on your own. I will stand by you with unconditional passion and compassion in your exploration; I will hold you accountable, provide you with unique viewpoints to consider, and most importantly offer actionable tools and grounded questions to guide you to your own answers.

These stories demonstrate what is possible when you intentionally set down your status quo to consider what is true for you. An Olympic athlete seeks a trainer not because she is incapable of training but because she desires accountability, perspective, feedback, and tools to add to her toolbox. Take a breath and prepare to receive your toolbox for deep, vulnerable, and transformative internal work.

Your 10,000-Foot View

The Alignment Journey is the process of calling forth your true values, desires, beliefs, blind spots, and fears. The Alignment Journey will provide not only encouragement, greater understanding, and inspiration to pursue your best life but empowering action steps for you to live it.

Personalize this book by comparing your own experiences to the real-life examples I share from clients' and my own Alignment Journeys. Then take courageous action to enact your discovered alignment—no matter how uncomfortable the ride may be.

While the outcome of the Alignment Journey is, in fact, what I hear many of you seeking—a meaningful life of purpose, fulfillment, and happiness—the process is full of surprises.

I've already declared a unique boundary between my expertise and your own: I am not your answer or wise guru. I am your guide, mirror, and coach to aid in your own discovery and remind you of your innate capability to thrive.

I am your companion, as well. I, too, have courageously lived through each stage of the Alignment Journey—many times. I, too, have contemplated crossroads between comfortable, shiny, and rewarded success versus the alternative I knew to be best for me. I deeply understand the turbulence that can accompany a life of alignment. Sometimes, steps and leaps of faith toward alignment feel scary as hell. They may even introduce world-shattering heartbreak. Because of this, you may at times doubt yourself, doubt me, or doubt the worth of this journey. Yet I know this journey is worth everything… and you will soon see why.

The Alignment Journey focuses on a research-based, experience-backed perspective that a meaningful life of purpose, fulfillment, and happiness rests in your ability to be with all experiences fully. Too often we limit our feelings, outcomes, and experiences to a dichotomy of negative versus positive. It is rarely so.

We are conditioned to view success as a direct, predictable, and therefore replicable journey. My experience as an individual, positive psychology scholar and coach suggests the journey to authentic success is cyclical and dynamic. Therefore, although the Alignment Journey is written in chronological order, please keep in mind it is anything but linear; further, it is not one singular ride, but many in a lifetime.

My First River: Saying "Heck No!" to My PhD

Like a good student, I sat tall in my chair behind one of six tables placed in a U around the lab. My new colleagues settled in on my right and left, and sunlight poured through the windows around what used to be a living room. The mountains beyond those windows reminded me how far I was from home.

We were only a few months into the program, yet I felt confident enough to name the professor who led today's discussion as my favorite. She, too, had called the Midwest home at one point in time—and unlike other academics, she didn't hide her life outside of work. She often spoke about her kids, who we had the pleasure to meet one afternoon, and she recognized opportunities to incorporate the world beyond stacks of literature, like the day she led us on a nearby waterfall hike.

Admittedly, I could see my life turning out to be quite similar to hers. At least, I hoped it would. Maybe that's why her comment felt so astonishing.

As in all cohort meetings, we took turns that day to ask questions about our expectations as PhD students in the positive developmental psychology program. This was our safe space to share anything on our mind.

"It is impossible," I began to illustrate proudly, "to simultaneously prioritize course requirements, lab hours, and the completion of independent research while personally adopting the very topic we study: a balanced and fulfilling life. So what should we prioritize?"

I felt hopeful my professor had an insight I was simply unaware of that would resolve the overwhelming tension I felt in the program. Instead, she laughed. The entire room laughed.

At first, I thought they were on my side—the kind of laughter that says, "Ah, yes. I feel that, too." But the silence that followed told me otherwise.

This moment of silence transported me back in time. Ironically, a few months earlier, I had sat in the exact same chair and asked a similar question to one of the founders of positive psychology. I had recently been accepted into the PhD program but had not yet committed; I had seriously considered other options for my post-undergraduate move during my weeks spent on the program's waitlist.

This is what led me to ask Mihaly Csikszentmihalyi if I could perhaps delay my admittance to the program for one year.

I did not notice the shock around the room until my mom described it later that day. In fact, I didn't even realize it was a bold question to ask; I simply considered aloud one of many alternative possibilities for the coming year. I suppose questioning the order of life is a pretty big deal in a room full of high-achieving rule-followers.

Inevitably, I chose to enroll in the PhD program that year, but it was not as obvious of a choice as I had anticipated it to be when I applied. In my present moment, I was reminded why.

I watched my favorite professor reply to my question of balance through jaded eyes: "Everything is priority."

I tilted my head to the right with inquiry; making "everything" a priority was an impossible ask. But my heart dropped as I realized my own clarity was not mirrored in the eyes of my colleagues—colleagues who were quickly becoming close friends. I felt confused as I looked around the room to witness expressions of agreement, rather than outrage. Were my peers willing to sacrifice their own well-being to make it through this program?

Their accepting responses prompted me to take pause, again, and consider if I would be willing to make the sacrifices this type of expectation asked of us. I reexamined the projector screen to my left that displayed our anticipated timeline to obtain a PhD: seven years.

No effing way.

I left the psychology lab that day feeling hurt and betrayed. I questioned my original assumption that my favorite professor in this program was, in fact, balanced between academia, purpose, and personal fulfilment. I reflected on our conversation about running a few weeks ago. "I was the healthiest I've ever been during graduate school," she beamed. At the time, I nodded in agreement. I, too, was committed to a strict workout regimen to relieve the stress of school. Now, I wondered if our shared commitment to fitness signified wild imbalance rather than health.

My head spun as I walked down the sidewalk, sweat dripping down my back from the ninety-degree California heat—or maybe this was my body's natural response to my crumbling plans. I tried my best to make sense of a program that blatantly encouraged its students to do the exact opposite of what we learned in class.

In consideration that one of the most powerful figures in the field of positive psychology was the leader of this program, and knowing this was the only PhD program for positive psychology in the United States... I started to question the field as a whole. If individuals closest to this topic could not follow the advice of our research in their own lives, was the field itself an illusion? If we, the leaders and future of this field (or so they told us during our welcome assembly) cannot align with what we know is necessary to foster a life of well-being—why the hell are we studying, writing books, and lecturing about it?

What followed this conversation was a year-long internal debate, led by myself and supported by countless coaches, friends, and mentors. I could either continue on my original path to earn a PhD in positive developmental psychology or switch programs during my second year of graduate school and leave with a master's degree in positive developmental psychology with an emphasis in evaluation.

A year and a half after hearing my favorite professor's response to priorities, I walked across the graduation stage to accept my master's degree. That moment stands as one of my proudest accomplishments. Not so much because I had earned my graduate degree—though I am proud of that, as well—but because I courageously said no to a shiny, misaligned alternative.

Receiving my master's degree also stands as one of my first acts of authentic alignment in my adult life, and it would set the tone for many more. With time, I came to understand pushback, difficulty, and discomfort as data points to consider rather than signs I am on the wrong path. I have come to accept I may be the only voice in the room that questions the rules, and while I still strive to pause and consider whether my immediate instincts are unfounded, I often find they are not.

I am an ambitious rule-follower at heart, but I've learned I have a prerequisite for rule-following: I must understand and agree with why. In doing so, I have also empowered myself to learn I have my own rules to follow. (You do, too.)

My Mountain: Saying "Heck Yes!" to Coaching

Growing up, my parents set a rule that food must be eaten in the kitchen. Maybe we could have predicted my graduate school defiance the day Mom found my four-year-old butt sitting with her bowl of cereal on the line where our living room carpet met our kitchen tile.

Questioning is my status quo—which is both a strength and shortcoming. I recognize it can be beneficial, at times, to simply do as I am told. Simultaneously, questioning supported my pathway to authentic alignment by age twenty-five rather than pursuing that PhD and inevitably experiencing a midlife crisis.

As I naturally and intently questioned the status quo from afar, I witnessed a common experience—and it all starts, in metaphor, with a river of individuals just like me.

The river itself is the rulebook, passed down from generation to generation. It has the ability to foster good things: fertile soil, a fun ride, and efficient travel all the way from a mountain's peak to a beautiful ocean sunset: success.

Although it is not inherently bad or wrong, it is not the only path. We have labeled the river as the only path: the right, smart, best choice.

The river's current picks up momentum and smooths edges that previously provided opportunity for pause as more individuals adopt this singular pathway. Alternative mountains, trails, valleys, swamps, fields of luscious green grass, inland lakes, and forests seem to not only be forgotten by most but labeled as unrealistic, naive, and stupid.

When I first depicted this river metaphor, I observed where I would land if I surrendered alongside my well-intended, rule-following colleagues: the ocean sunset. The destination was beautiful. The ride felt inviting, as well—especially as I considered my innertube of luxuries, safety nets, and friends along the same journey as I. To be clear, some individuals in this river and upon reaching their sunset destination seemed content—happy, even.

But I knew, in my core, I was not called to the river ride nor the sunset destination.

With this in mind, I at first could only imagine one of two alternatives. The first: to join the group of individuals who choose to accept good-enough happiness on an okay journey toward a beautiful, but personally undesired, destination. The second: to join the group of individuals I witness fighting like hell upstream—recognizing, out loud, their disapproval of the status quo. But even they continued to reside in the river, and wasn't it possible to escape it?

When I imagined myself in either scenario, I felt emptiness.

Whatever guidance there is in this world—the universe, god, intuition, human intellect—I am extraordinarily grateful I was led to coaching. In the world of coaching, my questioning mind thrived.

I believe I would have fallen into one of those two modes of being, the unfulfilled hard worker or the directionless drifter, had it not been for coaching. Life coaching was my opportunity to go in, to explore curiosities and questions, to consider possibilities in a space I felt secure, held, and alive. Coaching was my foundation when everything I knew vanished.

Coaching inquiries ranged from spontaneous to "I've been reflecting on this for three years, and I still cannot see clearly…" I sent messages to my coach when I could not voice my truth to my significant other. I rehearsed resignations from jobs. I sent celebratory dance videos in anticipation of the beauty I had experienced. I quit my PhD.

Coaching was accountability to live the life I desired rather than the one I felt captured by. Through coaching, I realized I did not have to follow the river rulebook—or if I was more comfortable with a rulebook, I could write my own. Of greatest magic, coaching led me to you.

I am in awe of my current life: it is authentic, true, expansive, and magical—and to no surprise, it is not the prescribed river.

Now it is your opportunity to nourish deep understanding, trust, and courage in yourself. Outlining the Alignment

Journey is my passionate service to aid you to discover your own possibility, be it in the mountains, the valley, or the river itself.

WHAT ABOUT YOUR NEXT LIFE WOULD BE DIFFERENT?

As a final note of preparation for your challenging yet rewarding journey ahead, let's return for a moment to where we began: If you speak to your most glorious life and greatest alignment, only to dismiss it with statements, such as "maybe in my next life…" I counter: What would be different?

What would be different in your next life? Would you have more courage? Would you give yourself permission? Would you make different choices earlier in life? Would you courageously follow your heart instead of your wallet, or your fears, or society's expectation?

Because if it was truly your next life, I predict you would feel exactly the same as you do in this moment: you would long for something specific, just as you do now. You would be scared, overwhelmed, or unwilling to rock the boat.

I predict in your next life, you would choose the safe route, too—because in your next life, you would still be you.

I see the child inside you, dreaming great dreams; I see your instincts that long to align you with your soul and passion and greatest potential on this earth.

My heart aches for you to say "maybe in this life"—and as you give yourself a chance, I feel the entire world shift in preparation for your true arrival.

Maybe, in following your beam of light, you will feel more alive than you ever have before. Rather than abiding by the belief that it is too late or you are too old, you can shine with gratitude for your most full years of life yet to be experienced.

At any moment, of any day, you can choose to begin your next life. So why not begin today?

"Maybe in this life. Maybe now."

Your Alignment Journey Map

The Alignment Journey is a process of becoming aware, considering new perspectives, and being in the experiment of your own life to discover your truth and act accordingly. For greater understanding and remembrance, I interweave the already introduced river metaphor throughout the stages of your Alignment Journey.

Chapter 1: Lost in the River. The introduction illuminated the underpinning *why* behind the Alignment Journey. I set a foundation of encouragement, explanation of coaching, and a piece of my own story to hint at the ride you are about to venture.

Chapter 2: Find Your Compass. Because I do not know what's best for you, I cannot say "move to the left" or "let's get out of the river and explore this jungle instead." Rather, I will lead you to find and foster the compass that guides your entire Alignment Journey experience: you.

Chapter 3: Float to the Riverbank. With your compass in hand, I lead you to create space for its use. This is your opportunity to step aside from the river, maybe for the first time, and give power to your personal truth.

Chapter 4: Observe Your Surroundings. With space to recognize your internal observations, emotions, and desires, you experience clarity and understanding. Your eyes open to the limitless possibilities amid the landscape around you.

Chapter 5: Set Your Direction. With new insights and opportunities comes discomfort. Pause and feel what precedes your first major alignment shift—anticipation before you begin to hike from river to mountain peak.

Chapter 6: Start Walking. With a trusted foundation of space, clarity, and direction, you are ready to act. This may mean packing your bag, drawing a map, or touching the mountain slope; even one small step of alignment promises significant benefit.

Chapter 7: Embrace Your Switchbacks. The Alignment Journey is dynamic and full. Climbing a metaphorical mountain will include ups and downs. You may grieve the river or feel frustrated about your course, as well as sing in celebration and rest in contentment.

Chapter 8: Enjoy the View. Taste what it feels like to celebrate living in alignment with who you really are, what you truly want, and what you ultimately believe in. Stand upon your lookout with pride and admiration for the journey that brought you here.

Chapter 9: Discover More. Sometimes, there's another mountain. Or you get lost in another metaphorical river. Or maybe the earth shakes and your foundation cracks below you. There is always more, and this is good news.

Chapter 10: Ready Enough. I send you off with notes of motivation and love. You have everything you need, including my and others' relentless support, and you are ready enough to continue endless journeys of grand, rewarding alignment.

CHAPTER 2

Find Your Compass:
Who Are You Listening To?

In the pursuit of a good life, you encounter an overwhelming amount of solutions:

> *Change your diet. Monetize your passion. Get a degree with the highest income potential. Take a vacation. Work harder. Read this book. Do as [this successful person] did. Listen to your elders. Follow your gut. Attend this workshop. Receive your degree(s). Drop out like Bill Gates! Get fit. Embrace your body. Invest in yourself. Avoid debt. Meditate. Fall in love. But love yourself, first.*

Between social media, personal development courses, magazines, inspirational speakers, colleagues, and family—you may feel paralyzed by the amount of advice thrown your way. It is not uncommon to get caught in the trap of analysis paralysis—trying to gather and scrutinize this advice to find the *best, right* answer.

To some degree, this is a helpful practice... but only to some degree.

Trust me, I love a good research base to support opinions, practices, and guidance. In my professional training as an evaluator, I learned firsthand the benefits of building programs, organizing systems, and making decisions grounded in research. Moreover, I witnessed the detrimental outcomes from programs, systems, and decisions built on wishful thinking, assumptions, and no research whatsoever.

It can be useful to turn to experts and learn from others' lived experiences, but how much weight do you place here? Even more, how much room do you leave for your *own* expertise and lived experience?

YOUR VOICE MATTERS

You heard the story of my four-year-old self eating her cereal at the very edge of the kitchen. At that age, I didn't understand the consequences of spilling my Reese's peanut butter puffs on new carpet—nor did I care; I wouldn't be the one cleaning up my mess nor forking over the money for a deep clean of our living room.

When our brain is not fully developed and we do not completely understand the world around us, we rely on our parents and teachers to advise almost every move. There comes a point, however, when we learn the essentials and need less guidance.

Consider our journey as passengers in a car: we transition from baby carrier to car seat to booster seat, then to riding in the back, the front, and eventually driving ourselves. But this metaphor doesn't fit when it comes to our approach for making life decisions. Why?

We start, necessarily, by listening to advice and guidance from our parents and babysitters. Then, we transition through our friends, teachers, professors, and boss. Next, we turn to research, movies, self-help books, therapists, and the successful 1%.

Rather than guiding ourselves from car seat to driver, we tend to assume someone else knows better than we do—always. This simply can't be true for a world full of individuals with unique lived experiences. Furthermore, even experts have personal experiences that filter their focus, and even your parents have not lived your life, in this generation, with your unique preferences, interests, and opportunities.

I often hear intuition-based decision-making brushed aside as woo-woo. Historically, I brushed my own gut feelings aside, as well. Like the time I accepted a position working as an evaluator even after I had decided to begin my own business, instead. (I quit the evaluation gig three months later.)

Science, facts, and expert opinions can feel certain and, thus, foster a feeling of safety and confidence. But what determines certainty when making decisions for your individual life?

During graduate school, I was enveloped in research— something I historically assumed to be true. What I learned is researchers must have significant findings for their data to be of any value and the work to be considered for publication. This bias leads to the file drawer problem, by which thousands and millions of insignificant research studies seemingly don't exist and are unavailable for others to learn from.

Understanding the imperfection in research created just enough space in my mind to consider *more* than external data and others' expert opinions. This is not to say research itself is to be ignored entirely—rather, there is room for my own critical thinking even in the face of research-based evidence.

Similar realizations broadened my decision-making processes when I started asking *why* and *where* my heavily weighted external advice originated.

My undergraduate professor told me I would not get into a PhD program. Why? Because she had multiple examples from her experience as an advisor that admittance was difficult, especially for someone who did not have much research experience—someone like me. In hindsight, of course, her experiences did not accurately predict my own PhD admittance.

To this day, my dad mentions the importance of building my resume. Why? Because in his experience, resumes are consequential for employment—and employment, in his experience, is a successful avenue to income and a good life. (That does not mean there are no other avenues to success and a good life. In fact, I am living an alternative variation as we speak.)

Advice and guidelines I used to consider *fact* may be more accurately described as others' personal experiences. That does not mean they are false, nor does it mean you must ignore data, research, evidence, and others' opinions and experiences altogether.

Read the signs. Pause for a moment to consider their truth. You may have a coach who knows all about your values, dreams, fears, and beliefs—so you are not only guided through your critical thinking process but have an objective, trained voice to point out any blind spots you do not see yourself.

Ultimately, and simply, just give your own experiences and intelligence a little more benefit. Gift your own voice a little more weight.

WHEN A TRAIL SIGN SAYS DANGER

One spring afternoon, my dog, Aatto, and I were walking our usual route around the lake when I noticed a sign placed in front of the water: "KEEP OFF. Dangerous. Ice not safe." My eyes took in the warning and then glanced behind it to the soft lake waves crashing on the beachfront.

Imagine you, too, are standing before this lake; you come upon this sign on a warm spring day and read its cautionary message. What would you think?

Would you avoid the lake because there must be ice if the sign says so? Would you laugh at the sign's inaccuracy? Would you consider the city workers who placed this sign wrong or stupid because there is no ice to be seen?

Of course not. Just as I did, I bet you would read the sign and understand it as outdated. You would quickly piece together the sign was meant for the winter season and simply has not been removed since the spring thaw.

Thus, it is possible to use your own critical thinking skills in the midst of external, professional advice. Furthermore, you can do this without judgment, struggle, or doubt— because no external thing understands yourself, has gone through your unique experiences, and knows what is best for you better than *you*.

This is what I invite you to do, far more often, and in all aspects of your life.

To repeat, again and again: I do not have your answers. You do. I am your guide to help *you* unveil your own answers and courageously act in alignment.

Practice One: Ignite Your Voice

If you're feeling scattered and overwhelmed, you may be focused on someone else's answers: You did as your parents instructed. You followed the guidance of your teachers. You were an A+ student and employee of the month.

This mode to success is what you are taught because this is how you survive as you develop from a child to an independent adult. But now, you are in a new stage of development and upleveling, which requires a new level of understanding and learning.

Take a courageous moment to ask yourself: What does success mean to *me*? What do *I* desire? What do *I* care about? What makes *me* happy? How do *I* want to get there?

Maybe you've never heard your own voice amid the noise, within the river. Maybe you heard it but suppressed it—or feared it or thought it was stupid. Maybe you followed it, once—or a few times—only to be told by someone else that it wasn't realistic or that another way was best... so you continued checking those darn boxes.

Whatever your past story is with your voice—you have the power to choose a new story today, tomorrow, and every day moving forward. Dare to begin again.

LISTEN TO YOUR DISCOMFORT

When you start to tune into your own voice, especially if you have not adopted this practice much in your life prior to this point, you are bound to find some uncomfortable truths. This, especially, is when to tune in and listen.

My newest client and I were two minutes into her first coaching session. I sat on the couch in her office adjacent to her desk. She sat in her office chair. To kick off our first session, I asked something along the lines of "What called you to coaching?"

She began apologetically. "Well... I just feel like... life should be good; life IS good. Business keeps me busy, I'm studying work I'm excited about, I have amazing friends, my boyfriend and family are wonderful... Everything is fine! But I..." Tears rolled down her cheeks. They would be the first of many during our sessions together. "I'm sorry, I don't know why I'm crying."

As I write these words, I'm smiling. I can still picture her in her professional chair in front of her laptop with the most color-coordinated calendar I've ever seen. And at the time, although she was blowing her nose and wiping tears from her cheeks, she was laughing, too—because in those early moments together as coach and client, our souls connected. She let me in, and I saw who she really was.

It was the beginning of a coaching relationship that would span nearly two years. I coached her through graduate school, launching her six-figure business, moving across the country, and becoming engaged to her partner. We co-experienced many beautiful events, celebrations and loss, profound insights, and all the waves that accompany an upleveled life. By our third coaching contract, she said, "I don't know if I could trust anyone more than you."

This statement feels beautifully ironic when I return to the scene from our first session. At one point, we were on the floor (as goes with coaching), and I invited her to venture deeper into the sadness that had surfaced. I can still picture her questioning eyes looking back at me to ask: "Why? What's the benefit of doing that?"

In all my work as a coach—and in my work as a client—I recognize a natural resistance to uncomfortable, "negative" emotions. We fear they will last forever. We worry we will never get out of the deep dark hole if we let ourselves go there. We fail to understand their significance by giving them labels such as unhelpful or weak. We assume it's better to focus on the positive—or in my case, historically speaking, I thought I could logic my way *out* of discomfort.

Yet, in all my work as a coach (and absolutely in my work as a client) I've learned just how vital it is to welcome what's uncomfortable. Not doing so limits your understanding of what's really going on—of the core issues, beliefs, values, and stories that guide your life whether you bring awareness to them or not. Furthermore, in my experience, if you turn down your negative emotions and experiences, you inevitably turn down the good. And ultimately, well-being is the ability to be with *all* of your thoughts, emotions, and experiences.

I do not deny the discomfort of letting in the hurt, sadness, loss, anger, and grief. (Though, in my experience, emotions pass far quicker when you fully let them in.) You may seek additional support to navigate your experiences in a healthy and safe way, *and* I invite you to adopt a new perspective about discomfort altogether. Discomfort is the untapped shortcut to your answers and wisdom; discomfort is your strength—not your weakness. And ignoring discomfort is your Achilles' heel.

Have you felt those little knocks at your door? The call to pursue a different path? The signs that something is off?

Have you ignored them because "I should be grateful for what I have" or because you assume "this is just how life goes"? Or are you living in the camp of "maybe once I [fill in the blank], it will all be worth it"?

Even if your current reality is unsatisfactory, stressful, or obviously out of alignment with what is best for you, do you put your blinders on and keep working because you are not willing to risk a *new* type of discomfort?

If so, notice my final statement: "a new type of discomfort." If you resonate with any of the questions above, you are already uncomfortable. Your life may feel empty—no matter how much stuff or people you have around you. You may be searching to no avail for meaning and purpose. You may realize you feel an insatiable longing for *more*. This is where to begin your experiment with discomfort. Get curious about the discomfort that already exists in your life to lessen the fear you have around the discomfort you project into your future.

Just as my client asked during our first session together, you may push back: What's the benefit of feeling my "bad" feelings? To reiterate, this is often where your most true, concise wisdom resides for what you deeply desire in life. Second, I contend these are not bad feelings but simply feelings. These are aspects of life that, when used, help you experience more of your life—rather than detract from life.

If those answers don't convince you to feel your present discomfort, consider this: inviting discomfort into your life will not only prevent your own self sabotage; the vulnerability, honesty, and growth that follows your exploration with discomfort will also stop you from damaging the life of everyone around you.

BREAK FREE FROM SELF-MADE PRISONS

As you know, I eventually left my positive psychology PhD program—but before I had the clarity and courage to do so, I was living in a world of shoulds.

I regularly felt guilt for spending my time on anything unrelated to school. I felt overwhelming stress with the demands placed on us by the university. I felt angry at everyone else, who was "making" me work on my thesis instead of encouraging a much-needed break.

Furthermore, I was fighting for my own suffering because I'd worked hard to achieve *success*: I was earning a decent wage, I had fancy clothes and intelligent friends, and I looked toward a predictable path ahead...

I knew I felt imbalanced and unhappy, but when I considered what it took to get me there, and what opportunities might lie ahead if I were to persevere, I felt it might be worth it. My internal dialogue called me entitled and told me to be grateful.

Another motivator to maintain my current trajectory was my denial that my dissatisfaction had anything to do with those around me. In fact, I thought it was better for those around me if I maintained what I knew was out of alignment for me; I was doing everyone a favor by following their rules, fulfilling their desires, and making *them* more comfortable. Assuming this was true, my own discomfort felt like an okay compromise to make.

I said, "maybe in my next life..." to my wild dreams. I decided to make it work. Keep my head down. Don't rock the boat.

But what happens when you hold a balloon under the water? *Whoosh.*

The pressure I felt from living in misalignment climaxed during a family ski vacation in the spring graduate school, year one. Although it was spring break, I had work to do, a thesis to write, and a paper to complete during our week in Colorado. I wanted to board on the slopes with my family. I wanted to go out to dinner at our favorite restaurant. I wanted to share a good conversation with my mom over a delicious cup of coffee.

I felt I couldn't. I didn't have permission. I didn't believe it was possible to complete the work I had in front of me and partake in family events. So I forced myself to stay inside our condo and work.

Anger and resentment about my current reality built until it overflowed with sobs on the living room armchair. My family had just walked out the door for dinner, and my entire being begged me to join them. Instead, I stared at my computer and mandated my fingers to type.

I didn't see another way. "I had to." "I don't have time." "This is what it takes."

In hindsight, I missed an entire family vacation that year. Sure, I was physically present, but my traditionally joyful spirit was not. This example is perfect to illuminate how your own combative internal world not only affects yourself but everyone else.

Because I was unhappy with my current work, because I continued to abide by rules I disagreed with, because I forced myself into a lifestyle and career trajectory that felt heavy rather than expansive, I was hindering my ability *and* my family's ability to thrive. In maintaining misalignment, I neglected trust, love, and goodness—with myself and with those I loved most.

Two years later, I rode down the stunning mountainside of Breckenridge alongside my family. I sipped coffee with my mom without concern for time or a lingering haze of stress. I fell asleep next to my wonderful partner, who joined us in Colorado for the first time, and I felt overwhelmingly grateful for the life I had *intentionally chosen* to live.

Our belief systems, stories of obligation, and fears of the unknown are powerful. I get how scary it is to go against the status quo or change paths. I know how uncomfortable it is to simply question the path you are on.

AND. As I sit here writing my first book, I must tell you: choosing a life of alignment is *worth* the effort. It is *worth* the discomfort. It is *worth* the reality checks and perspective shifts, the habit change and deep breaths, the coaching investments and intuitive trust. It is *worth* it because the process of alignment leads to wellness and life.

Alignment led to me, today, feeling proud and feeling alive.

Praise everything I challenged my original path. Praise everything I said yes to my own version of success and drew a hard boundary at anything that didn't align.

Praise everything you can, too.

CHAPTER 3

Float to the Riverbank: Create Space for Transformation

Difficulty, at some point, has become a prideful experience. We label hard work as the most valuable way to spend our time.

While the path to success, a life of fulfillment, and our own growth certainly includes some challenging experiences, what I witness is an absolute lack of the opposite: our ability to *be*.

This was strikingly obvious during my years as a yoga instructor. I was surprised to watch far more discomfort with students during postures of release instead of physically demanding postures. Lying still was the most uncomfortable of all. During final resting posture, akin to lying down to sleep at night, I consistently observed students wiggle in place or squint their eyes open to ensure they weren't supposed to be elsewhere.

During my years as an instructor, I also heard our bias toward hard work in the casual exchanges between students. One day after class, a young man told me he enjoyed his first yoga practice even though it felt challenging for him—to which his friend chuckled: "Wasn't it restorative yoga?"

Outside of the yoga studio, we furrow our brows and work twelve-hour days because it feels more comfortable to control than to trust. We manifest fears such as not doing enough, while it may be more accurate to fear we are doing too much.

Achievement and action are plastered across our billboards, within our offices, and in many self-development books. Thus, it is novel to consider that sometimes progress does not require you to crowd calendars, organize checklists, or master a skill. Because of this—because we are prone to action over rest—one of the most profound steps you will take in your Alignment Journey is step one: pause and create space for transformation.

Step one is wildly important, especially in an achievement-based society, yet if I read "create space" as step one in a process of any kind five years ago... I likely would have skipped ahead. I wouldn't blame you if that is your first thought, as well.

I pride myself in being an energetic action-taker. I value planning, productivity, and efficiency as some of my greatest strengths. It is often more comfortable for me to do than it is for me to be. But I came to learn comfort isn't always a fruitful guide.

I observed what happened when I or my clients continuously rushed to action. Without first creating space, we lost the opportunity to clarify next steps, understand current decisions, and trust the greater process. By failing to pause, our action was directionless.

So what's possible with pause? Ask my yoga student who had an epiphany to a year-old problem after just ten minutes in savasana. Ask my previous business coach, who reached her first six-figure year after working three days a week so she could enjoy life for four. Ask me, who recently danced around my kitchen table because I came up with a brilliant new idea for Yes&, my coaching business, after I took a break to color.

If you're still clutching the belief that challenge and action are always best, consider this: what if rest and allowing yourself to *be* is the most challenging thing you could do?

When I sense my clients are about to arrive at a moment of pause on their journey, I prepare myself to co-navigate fear, confusion, and a little bit of panic. Again, we live in a society that deems hard work as *the way*—the way to get things done, to grow, to become stronger, to experience success, to live. To suggest a step that opposes this approach is bound to fire up resistance. Rather than perceive your resistance as a roadblock, I invite you all to view it as a way in.

Your Breath's Secret Wisdom

Notice, for a moment, your breath. Sense your inhale and experience your exhale. (I'm serious… Pause, right now. Inhale and exhale.)

Now, notice the pause that exists after your inhale is complete and before your next exhale begins.

By nature, in your own breath, there is a moment where nothing needs to be done; there is no task nor required action besides the *absence* of work—nonetheless, this space of nothingness must exist.

To emphasize this point, try to "fix" or eliminate the pause in your breath; for a moment, remove the space between your inhales and exhales...

When you do so, you will immediately experience stress and exhaustion from forcing what is unnatural. If you do this for a prolonged period of time (which I do not recommend), you may even pass out.

The space between your breath is essential, and breath without space feels *bad*. Yet this is how so many of us walk around the world. We force decision after decision, and action after action. This is parallel to yelling at a tree to blossom immediately after its leaves have fallen—or as illustrated, parallel to removing the space between your breaths.

You may trick yourself into believing that removing space, expediting decisions, or prompting quick action accelerates your agenda. More often than not, it does the opposite.

What if *space* was your key to masterful decisions, powerful action, and ultimate success? Rather than forcing quick inhale after exhale, metaphorically or literally hyperventilating, I invite you to pause, instead.

Remember, there is nothing to *do* in this space of pause; the only point is for it to exist and for you to patiently exist in it.

If your mind fears this part of the cycle as being unproductive or unnecessary, return to your breath; notice the mandatory pause between every one of your inhales and exhales, and use this as assurance that pause is essential progress.

Take in the Scenery

If I were to introduce you to two individuals, one of whom worked three days a week and another who worked five, who would you assume is more productive? Alternatively, what if you worked seventy hours one week and twenty hours the next—which week would your boss applaud?

Our belief that working more equates to accomplishing more is simply that: a belief. Therefore, like any belief, this may be true, self-created, or blatantly false for your own life.

In graduate school, an advisor told me I was one of the most well-rounded students to enter the program. I believe her statement pointed to the fact that I intentionally turned down extra projects, reserved time for leisure (like taking voice lessons every Friday afternoon), and questioned university expectations that discouraged self-care.

Although I recognize graduate school to be an intentionally challenging endeavor, what struck me most about the mindset I encountered at my graduate institution was its direct opposition to the research and teachings in which we were involved, as introduced previously.

Every individual in my program was a positive psychology scholar. Thus, we knew precisely the elements required to live a good and well life—and working relentlessly to meet overwhelming expectations is not included in that formula.

It's not surprising to learn mental illness is disproportionately high for graduate students.

After surrounding myself in a stressed-out graduate school environment, one of my greatest takeaways was my determined stance to *live* positive psychology rather than grind myself down to study it. In hindsight, I think my tenacity to live was what my professor recognized as well-rounded.

Today, my schedule includes two days off per week—at the least. To clarify, these are not two days kind of off or "if I need to reply to one email that's okay" off… Two. Days. OFF.

Up until recently, these had been the hardest days of my week by far. Yet, just as I practiced balance in graduate school, I safeguard my rest absolutely.

To this day, my days off are the most valuable days of my week. I find myself bored and thus seek new hobbies. I go for a walk, witness the beauty of my city, and recognize a need in my community I had previously missed. I play my guitar and sing loud—practicing the courage I will use at my next presentation. I chat with a man in the grocery store for a half hour just because I have nowhere else to be, and we develop a valuable connection.

Yet even with abundant realized benefits, I am still actively shifting a historic mindset that I am lazy, missing productive time, or not enough because I have created space. Simultaneously, I actively fight the urge to work simply because I love what I do. Doing what I know is best for me holistically and long term pays off tenfold.

My energy and excitement about work—intentionally held back like water at a dam during my days off—releases in passionate fury my next workday. My productivity sky-rockets because I am not burned out and, in fact, desire to work. I've often jotted down tens of new ideas from my time outside of the office, and I accomplish them efficiently because procrastinating into the weekend isn't an option. Most importantly, my days off foster a fuller experience of my authentic life, within and beyond work.

I believe we all know, to some degree, how essential it is for humans to rest, whether we've studied it, experienced the benefits firsthand, or include rest in a siloed area of our life (for example, between sets at the gym). For even greater proof, the field of positive psychology highlights profound benefits for individuals who step away from work and *live*. Some experiences known to foster greater wellness and life satisfaction include time in nature, casual interaction with neighbors, intimate connection, physical activity, hobbies, creativity, and play!

So let's revisit your underlying assumption that elements involving rest and empty space are leisurely and insignificant—yes? Dare to question: is it, truly, more productive to work seven days than three? What if time off would foster greater productivity? Or digging even deeper, could it be that productivity is not your greatest value?

Space Practice One: Time Completely Off

Your first practice to create space is to take time off. I invite you to incorporate even one hour of complete off time into your week. Remain open to what you will experience in this hour: maybe you feel utter boredom, maybe you realize you're exhausted and decide to take a nap, or maybe you're antsy as heck and walk circles up and down your hallway. It's all good; it is all part of the experiment.

Use your off time to create an intentional space of curiosity around what your life is at its most foundational level. Who are you when you're not doing anything? Where does your mind go when there are no distractions? What piques your interest, and what do you avoid?

This may also illuminate a need in your life to seek support, and I highly encourage you to act on this instinct if it arises. Sometimes, especially if you haven't given yourself much space before, you discover a *lot* that has been hidden away—maybe for a long time. Therapists, coaches, healers, teachers, mentors, partners and family, friends, and courses can offer guidance and safety if it feels overwhelming to sit in space alone.

Need a pep talk to reset your mindset and take a day off successfully? I include a day-off pep talk in the Alignment Journey workbook, in addition to extra Create Space practices! Get yours at yesandbymarin. com/workbook.

CLARITY IS RIGHT IN FRONT OF YOU

I stared at the tree limbs that covered parts of the bright blue sky above me. I watched the leaves sway in the breeze and filled my lungs with fresh air. Any remaining stress was released with one big exhale. I realized I finally believed with sincerity what I had been telling myself for weeks: everything is going to be okay.

It was the end of my first semester of graduate school. Alongside my best friends, I had been working my tail off to finish papers, reports, presentations, and exams. Finals week would finally end with one last exam to be completed that afternoon. Unfortunately, this was the most stressful exam of all; it was a class many first year students failed.

The stress of the year knotted in my shoulders—which came to light when I called my mom: "Hey, could you mail me that heating pad?" My stress may have also provoked my untimely fever that kept me bedridden earlier in the week.

Somewhat recovered, and motivated at the horrendous thought of having to take this class again, I hunched over my Research Methods notes. My eyebrows scrunched tightly together, my box of Joe-Joes was nearly empty, and a fearful story raced in my mind about the significance of this test as it pertained to my greater life.

I had lost sight of the forest; I was so focused on this one tree. All I could see was the bark in front of my nose.

I lifted the weight of my head so it once again aligned atop my spine. I took a shallow breath and relaxed my eyes beyond my desk. In my line of sight, I saw my green yoga mat gently balanced against my bookshelf.

With only forty-five minutes until exam time, I threw my mat in my backpack and biked to a nearby park. I chose a strong tree to lay my mat beside and selected a twenty-minute yoga sequence on my phone.

Breathe...

Breathe...

Breathe.

Practice ended as it usually does, in final savasana—but when I fluttered my eyes open, I felt nothing like I usually did before a test. I had rediscovered my truth: a perfect balance between my absolute, universal expansion and the insignificance of any one moment as the defining factor of my entire life.

After welcoming space into my life, rather than studying for forty-five more minutes, I received an A on my exam—and this is not the point.

The true celebration was how I recognized my stress as self-induced, which meant my freedom was also in my control. I courageously acted in alignment with what I was intuitively called to: a green yoga mat, a much-needed pause, and a few deep breaths.

The celebration was how I came home to myself and, in turn, rediscovered my most trusted compass.

LISTEN CLOSELY TO WHAT IS UNCOMFORTABLE

Earlier, I shared the story of a client who cried during our first session together. She questioned why it was important to feel uncomfortable emotions and ultimately celebrated her tears and discomfort as part of the Alignment Journey. The truth is this story isn't uncommon.

Almost everyone I work with cries during their first coaching session. Some even cry during our initial coaching consultation—when we simply talk through whether coaching with me would be a good fit for them at this time.

I've come to welcome a similar pattern among anyone—no matter gender, age, or temperament.

The other individual and I exchange niceties before transitioning into a conversation of deeper connection. As we do, the space between our webcams or telephones shrinks; I intently focus on the words and feelings of the other. Sometimes, this level of vulnerability and presence alone elicits tears—to at last arrive in a space where it is safe and welcome to be just as you are. Sometimes, the tears come after we dig a little deeper, when my client responds to questions that unveil their untold story, fear, longing, wish, and greatest desire.

Almost everyone says they are surprised by their tears. I am not. Many individuals apologize. I remind them there is nothing to be sorry for; this is simply their truth coming to light at last. This is the weight that's rested on their shoulders finally lifting—or at least made to feel a little lighter with the support of someone else holding it with them.

The profound power of space, such a wildly underrated invitation.

If you have suppressed any emotions, experiences, or truths by busying your life, you may be unpleasantly surprised by what you encounter in your newly created space. You, too, may cry. This, especially, is when to tune in and listen.

Discoveries such as sadness, hurt, and lack of fulfilment will guide your next step and greater alignment just as much as your found experiences of excitement, joy, and peace. Discomfort in this space is expected because these discoveries are new and because they illuminate things you have intentionally or unintentionally ignored up until this moment.

Listen like you would to a child who does not yet know how to clearly articulate their desires and needs. What is the underbelly of your experience? What are your honest sensations, emotions, and truth?

Lean into what it feels like to be unsatisfied with your current life. Truly experience the heartbreak you've shelved for years. Get pissed off at your advisor who said you would never be good enough. Say "EFF YOU" to the colleague who shot down your grand idea.

Feel frustrated at how *hard* you've been working, at all the attempted solutions you've tried: you implemented the billionaire morning routine, you ate clean, invested in the retreat (plus seven others), earned another promotion, changed cities, and got your name on a plaque—or whatever recognition you thought would elicit a sensation of *making it*, your name written in stone as successful and good...

Feel how disappointing it is that, even after all of it, you're more scattered and overwhelmed than ever before. You are exhausted, unfulfilled, confused, and now, angry as hell! You're tired of working so damn hard... for what?! This?!

You may be years into a career and objectively successful when it comes to money, relationships, and the papers framed on your wall. You may have a perception that you're doing it right because the world applauds you. You may be rewarded for going above and beyond, saying yes when others take the easy way out.

Does any of this truly matter if, in pause and stillness, you still feel off?

That said, do not mistake negative sensations as a demand to burn down *everything* you have built or abandon all you are in this moment. Because as much as anger, disappointment, and confusion exist in *space*, so does joy.

As you create space, start to take notice when your eyes light up with elation and curiosity. Give yourself permission to get excited, dance along the sidewalk, become best friends with someone you just met, or order rollerblades even though you'd never considered the activity before.

Enjoy the delicious taste of oven-baked cookies you had time to make from scratch because you at last took your Saturday completely off. Strum the guitar even though you only know three chords—and sing your little heart out even if the gentleman on the other side of the park tilts his head at your rendition of "Rockin' around the Christmas Tree" on this warm summer day.

Paint, even if you have no intention to paint again. Follow your interest to a new cafe. Watch the clouds or meditate on a leaf dancing in the wind for an hour. Lose yourself in a book that captivates your heart. Buy new living room furniture because it would make your home feel pretty.

Just as much as you notice your discomfort, notice your love. Notice your joy. Notice the free flow of energy that's waiting to escape from your soul and shine over the world around you. Notice what makes you feel alive.

This is what's been missing. This is who you are. This is what it is to be.

Space Practice Two: Don't Explain

When I say "feel what you find," I do not mean "explain what you find." If you're anything like me, however, this may be difficult to differentiate.

For me, it can feel easier to talk about, rather than sit in, my experience. It often feels more natural to open an Excel spreadsheet, calendar, or journal to transform abstract sensations into those that are tangible. Likewise, it was more comfortable years ago for me to hire a coach to explore my post-graduation career instead of mourning the loss of a life-changing, beautiful relationship. Many of my clients also begin our work together with a specific, constructed focus—only for us to unveil the true work desired at their core.

Next time you notice yourself avoiding an experience, invite curiosity and presence, instead. What would happen if you paused your description of the current moment and simply experienced it?

Here is an example from a journal entry years ago as I started crying, to my surprise, mid-workday:

> "Tears well in the back of my eyes. It feels like a strong arm is pressing against the breadth of my chest, prompting heavy pressure directly under my collar bones. The rest of my body tingles. My vision takes in a lot of blankness: the solid green of my coffee mug, the white wall in front of me, the monotone kitchen table where my laptop rests...

I was avoiding this emotion a moment ago. I choose to dive in now. I trust whatever lesson, meaning, or significance is meant to come from this moment will be adopted without my analysis or interpretation.

I feel more focused, alive, and aware. I feel more at ease."

QUIT YOUR WAY TO FULFILLING SUCCESS

I once worked with a business mentor. Fifteen minutes into our first meeting, once I summarized what led me to open my coaching business, he made an observation: "So you're good at quitting."

I'm still not sure whether to take his words as complimentary or insulting—but still today I'd react the same. I tilted my head to the right, raised my eyebrows in surprise, and chuckled, "I suppose you're right!"

My first year of undergrad was spent at the University of Colorado Boulder as a dance major—until I realized the dance industry was not a good fit for my long-term health and desired lifestyle. So I quit.

After one semester as a premed student, considering my next best option was to follow in my father's footsteps, I learned I had surprisingly different interests than my dad. I quit. When I realized the speaking career of my chemistry professor intrigued me more than any of her chem lectures, I quit. After one year as a stressed-out PhD student, I quit.

When I read through the contract my advisor sent over two months into our evaluation project, only to see the project had been extended by two months and my pay reduced, I quit. After three months working my subsequent job that seemed ideal on paper but did not, in fact, provide the flexibility I needed to simultaneously build my business, I quit. After three years teaching yoga and only a few weeks after realizing it no longer excited me to prepare and lead classes, I quit.

My business mentor was right when he pointed out how many times I'd quit—but I contend we could flip his comment on its head. The only reason my story had an abundant list of things I'd quit is because there was one thing I *refused* to quit all along: my true alignment.

Some might read my quit list and call me silly for turning down opportunities that were right under my nose. (I certainly sent my poor parents on a ride of emotions as they watched their daughter continuously abandon "safe" alternatives.) I, too, believe every item on my quit list could have been a pathway to success: dancing as my passion-turned-career, medicine as my roadmap to financial security, a PhD program toward prestigious professorship, a post-grad gig worth thousands of dollars in income, a job that placed me in front of my ideal coaching clients, and the best-paying yoga gig in the Twin Cities.

I knew what I was saying no to. And while it was tempting, at times, to say yes to *good enough* for the sake that I would at least have a paycheck or a career that kind of aligned with what I desired, my vision was greater.

My quit list was made possible because I had created space; I created space to envision my most ideal life, I created space to feel whether my current experiences aligned with this vision, and I created space to ride the waves that inevitably followed saying no to what those around me labeled as *right* and *safe*.

Because of this, I quit confidently. I also said *yes*, confidently, to what mattered more than any paycheck, good-enough gig, or shiny opportunity. I created the opportunity and space for alignment to enter my life.

Space Practice Three: Make Your Quit List

Space is the essential element to propel your Alignment Journey; without space, there is no direction, clarity, digestion of your current experiences and emotions, or vision for what beauty is to come. Without space, there also is likely *not* a badass quit list.

Create space to write out your quit list. Celebrate what you've said no to for the sake of pursuing your alignment.

If you feel doubtful or lack confidence in your list, create space to first feel and envision what you deeply desire. What will you absolutely *not* quit?

Gain access to over thirteen additional practices for creating space by downloading your Alignment Journey workbook at yesandbymarin.com/workbook.

Chapter 4

Observe Your Surroundings: Clarify Your Truth

If you type "individual sees color for the first time" into your YouTube search bar, hundreds of heartwarming videos will load onto your screen.

Colorblind glasses were released to the public around 2012, and their popularity has grown ever since. When a colorblind person wears these glasses for the first time, the experiences from both the person with colorblindness and their families are overwhelming; emotions range from tears of joy to jumping with excitement to standing still in shock.

Putting on a pair of glasses is a perfect metaphor for the second stage in your Alignment Journey: clarity.

Unlike creating space, your previous step in the Alignment Journey, clarity can happen in what feels like an instant; many of my clients refer to this type of clarity as an aha moment. At other times, clarity is its own process: a matter of learning, understanding, deepening the understanding, trying on a new perspective, and, at last, feeling clear about the circumstance, choice, or experience in front of you. This second type of clarity is more like focusing a camera lens rather than putting on a pair of glasses and instantly seeing the vibrant world around you.

I started to paint the Alignment Journey story using a river metaphor. Step zero was the lost, scattered feeling akin to you drifting within the river. Step one was your courageous step out of the river to catch your breath and create space. You may be surprised at just how much you had been missing, unaware of, or naive to prior to these steps.

Now, after catching your breath, you start to notice the sound of birds chirping, the feel of your own heartbeat. You finally take pause to note the little things, like the clothing you wear, how you feel, and how you were feeling, in hindsight.

You feel dirt from the river's edge between your toes... You notice a prairie alongside the river and wonder if it's always been there... You see mountains off in one direction and a deep forest in the other... There is a beautiful blue sky above you. And when you look back to where you came from, you notice for the first time that there were others swimming, floating, and fighting in the metaphorical river—just like you.

To experience clarity is to wipe the dirt from your eyes, stand up, and not only grasp what exists beyond the river but consider your place in it. So far in your Alignment Journey, you have asked yourself to simply be. Now, as you naturally progress into the next season, you have an opportunity to see, to understand, and to reflect, as well.

Clarity, the second stage in the Alignment Journey, is your time to use the data you gathered upon creating space. This stage is when you will experience a deep understanding of where you are and where you came from; this is when you will realize *why* and *what* you desire.

Go as High and as Far as You Can

If you find yourself in the midst of a tsunami, the Red Cross suggests going as high and as far as you can; "if you can see the wave, you are too close for safety." Keep this metaphor in mind as you traverse clarity—and as one example of why this metaphor is so suitable for this stage of the Alignment Journey, I'll take you back in time with my beloved calendar.

My ambitious personality, just like anyone's strength, has both a light and shadow side. Ambition allowed me to build a business I am extremely passionate about. Ambition also pressured me to complete five days of work in three in preparation for a travel weekend years ago.

I rearranged my calendar with confidence. On the Sunday prior to my ambitious three-day week, however, a wave of stress overwhelmed me. Will I have to prioritize work over everything else I value? Why do I have so many projects? Am I good enough to get this all done!?

Talk about being too close to the tsunami for safety. I was in it that Sunday night; I could absolutely see the wave.

Fast-forward to the following evening: I sat on my yoga mat on the rooftop of my apartment, hands resting palms up to face the brilliant blue sky, my eyes closed, and my head tilted ever so slightly toward the setting sun.

At that moment, I had completed two weeks of blog content for Yes&, felt brilliant about the end products, and excitedly anticipated a call with my life coach—wherein I'd have the opportunity to not only prioritize but bask in the values I feared could get trampled by a busy work week. I released *how* it could all get done and adopted a perspective of trust—I trusted not only what I would accomplish, but what I would not.

My tsunami, or the river in this mini Alignment Journey, was my jam-packed workweek. My riverbank of space entered when I chose to do yoga on my rooftop. Observing my landscape with clarity occurred shortly thereafter, as I felt an overwhelming sense of gratitude, confidence, and safety.

Notably, my experience of clarity did not require avoiding or eliminating my tsunami (a busy three-day workweek) altogether. Rather, I used this disturbance as a *cue* for the practices I have in my toolbox to create space and, therefore, experience clarity.

Now, you have these tools, too.

Clarity Practice One: Become the Observer

Your first practice to experience clarity is an invitation to take a step back. This might mean taking a few breaths, intentionally opening or closing your eyes, changing location, moving your body, or zooming out from your daily calendar.

"If you can see the wave, you are too close for safety."

While this practice may feel quite similar to the first stage of your Alignment Journey, your intention here is different. This is your opportunity to not only create space but observe yourself within it.

How are you feeling? Are your values represented here? Was there a blind spot you missed?

If You Feel Dizzy

Clarity feels good. Think of a time you've experienced it yourself: you figure out which pipe the water is leaking from, you solve the mystery at the end of a movie, you fix the bug in your system, you finally translate what your neighbor was trying to say in a language you didn't understand...

The relief, power, and confidence that accompany clarity feel fabulous. Like my clients, you likely look forward to aha moments amid your journey more than moments of confusing inquiry. But clarity is not "it."

Like the adage, "life is about the journey, not the destination," it is worth reminding yourself that clarity is *one* part of your Alignment Journey. Furthermore, clarity is often a journey itself.

I once heard growth referred to as a spiral (we'll explore this more in chapter eight); although we are always growing, we may revisit certain aspects of our life, beliefs, and lessons. This means, even if you thought you'd gotten over challenges from your past, you may revisit them from a new perspective or at another level.

I often find with my one-on-one clients that clarity leads to *more* questions... and thus, more growth. Here is an example of a growth spiral full of clarity:

"I'm feeling overwhelmed!"
Why, and for how long have I been feeling this way?

"Ohhh, because I feel pressured to get this promotion."
What do I assume this promotion would provide?

"I'm carrying an old story that money equals safety!"
Where did this story come from, and do I believe it?

"My grandpa... this belief isn't mine! I don't even like my job."
Is this job worth keeping so I feel safe?

"Ohhh, wait. I already feel safe!"
So... do I have to change anything?

"Well, I do want to spend more time outdoors!"
Does being outdoors require me to quit my job?

"Nope. I have a hike planned this weekend!"

These layers of clarity could go on forever—and that's the good news. As outlined in this example, there are also different types of clarity: realization that you'd been listening to external pressure or another person's opinion, remembering something about yourself, seeing an external circumstance more clearly, or understanding what brought you to your current experience. Likewise, the expression of clarity ("ohhh!") can be said in many different tones: excitement, shock, dread, humility, pride, relief, exhaustion, laughter...

Although clarity may look like an endless spiral with many types and experiences of clarity therein, it does not need to feel overwhelming or scattered.

One of my favorite activities to complete with new clients is to meet their self-caricatures. I invite my clients to explore different parts of themselves—the go getter, the daughter, the businesswoman, the loving child, the princess, the entitled ego, the jokester, the questioner, the planner, the broken hearted... With each caricature, we sit in a new seat, take on a new posture, and express unique statements with different tones in our voice.

I find that inviting abundant caricatures to the playing field fosters a deeper and clearer understanding of oneself. Furthermore, this activity creates a little space between one's identity as a whole and the individual aspects of ourselves, which invites conversation to take place without judgment and, therefore, with more space and clarity.

In one hour, I listen to my clients' transformation from feeling lost to understanding who they are, why they are, and how they choose to relate with their newly uncovered stories, beliefs, values, and personalities.

Then, just like the upward clarity spiral, it gets even better.

In the weeks, months, and years following our caricature session, our relationship and understanding of each caricature deepens; we understand where each caricature originated, what they're pissed about, what they desire, why it matters, what they sound like, when they're happy and when they want to sabotage the whole game. More caricatures come into play, too.

With time, my clients learn how to *be* with all aspects of themselves. My clients tell me how they're doing based on who is in charge, out of alignment, or needing attention. We laugh when that one caricature always butts its head when we're about to take a big leap, and they grow more compassionate with themselves as we *speak to* these traits rather than smother their requests.

Clarity Practice Two: Journal Your Caricatures

Your second clarity practice will help you explore your clarity spiral with understanding and humor. To start, get curious about the different parts of you. Then, make each part a cute, scary, and funny caricature. What is their name? What do they sound like? What is their favorite movie? Who do they hang out with? What do they do when they're mad? If they had one wish, what would it be?

Get creative and stay open-minded. One of my client's caricatures is a chill artist wearing Doc Martens and ripped jeans with a tattoo that says "Chill the f@ck out."

As you get to know them, also give yourself permission to draw boundaries. One of my clients pictured all of her caricatures in a (very entertaining) conference room. She, as her whole, higher self, always remained at the head of the table—unless she gave another caricature permission to take lead.

Do what is best for you, make it fun, and enjoy clarity on the other side.

For more on creating caricatures, check out my YouTube video from May 4, 2021: "Stop Your Mind from Spinning Through Caricature Development."

ASK THE HARD QUESTIONS

The plane rumbles down the jetway, shaking hundreds of individuals and our luggage overhead. I read a book—my preferred mode of distraction, second only to my John Mayer playlist. The individual to my right closes her eyes to sleep, the man to my left begins a movie on his phone.

"How interesting," I think, "the innumerable ways we find to distract ourselves—to cope with anxiety, fear, and discomfort…"

Then my own words hit me in the forehead. Just a few hours earlier, I posted a quote to my Instagram that read: "To end suffering, experience pain." I invited the Yes& community to welcome in emotions and fully experience their present moment in all its complex, uncomfortable, and pleasurable glory. Yet on this plane when I ask myself, "Am I experiencing my present moment?" my honest answer is no.

I am trying to avoid feeling fear—which feels amplified because this flight is out of my control. When I allow myself to tune into my present experience, even for a second, my mind races: What if we crash? What if a wing falls off? What if that little hole in the window becomes a big hole and blasts oxygen-deprived air through the side of the plane?!

Clearly, my current thoughts and relevant emotions are uncomfortable. And walking my own talk, I know how important, impactful, and life changing it is to fully experience what exists in the present moment, nonetheless.

I take a deep breath. I stop reading my book. I choose to lean into the discomfort.

I feel my heart, body, and mind slowly open to what exists under my avoidance and distraction. I welcome my fear in, I welcome my emotion and current experience—and I embrace it.

I am afraid. "What if I die?"

Oof... The fear sits in my chest like a heavy boulder. It's an ugly dark brown, or army green. I notice the fear drains my energy rather than adds to it. "What if all the parts on this plane fall apart and we crash?"

I continue to sit with my fear and remain curious. Then, I experience a simultaneous feeling of familiarity and surprise: my fear that at first felt incredibly powerful and overwhelming is now, naturally, transforming into wisdom.

I follow the admittedly daunting questions posed by my fears ("What if I die? What if the wing falls off? What if we lose oxygen?") and realize my response to each is quite simple: "Well... that'd stink."

"But what if I die on this plane, without control over my destiny?" "Well, that'd be a big bummer!"

And that's it. It'd stink. It would be a big bummer. Yet there's nothing I can do about the situation—nor is it a plausible outcome.

Staying present, I feel the fear dissipate.

Still, knowing I am out of control remains uncomfortable. To relate with this strong desire, rather than suppress it, I question where I am in control: within my own mind.

I have already embraced control by choosing to experience my fear. I am in control by choosing how to relate to this moment. I am in control by choosing which perspectives to adopt.

With a control list outlined, I revisit my fear of death as I watch the ground beneath us shrink. What is the significance of this fear?

It only takes a moment to discover an incredible nugget of insight: fearing death is the same thing as desiring life. I desire a full, authentic life experience. Of course! Further, I realize, I am experiencing my full, authentic life by choosing to embrace my current fearful moment.

By fully leaning into my current experience even though it was uncomfortable, I am reminded of one of my greatest values: I desire to live fully. Even better, I realize I had the opportunity to enact this value in the present moment on this plane.

Profoundly, by fully embracing my present discomfort, I not only faced my fear—I overcame it.

CONSIDER 50/50 SUCCESS

In a podcast episode, Brooke Castillo of The Life Coach School suggested life is always 50/50—always 50% positive and 50% negative. Although this is solely a hypothesis, my experiment adopting this belief has been empowering and freeing for myself and many of my clients.

If life is always 50/50, there is no pressure to be perfect, happy, or comfortable all of the time. Furthermore, as I've said before, my version of success is to be present and open to all experiences—to enjoy the bad just as much as the good—because, ultimately, I am confident and proud of the life I have *chosen* to live.

With this in mind, consider the discomfort you feel right now—the lack of fulfillment, frustration, longing, loss… Do you choose this to be your 50% negative experience? When you consider the positives in your life at the moment, do you choose those, as well?

Or is there a positive you've been called to for years—but you've suppressed it for whatever reason(s)? Is there a negative experience that may feel scary (e.g., financial uncertainty)—but also feels worth it, when you consider its correspondence to your dreams?

You are beyond capable of going after whatever you set your mind to. You are intelligent, hard-working, and well-intentioned. Furthermore, you are deserving, just as everyone else is, to live a life you're proud to call your own. And it is fully possible for you to feel fully alive, energized, content, abundant, and, truly, successful.

If you feel discomfort, this is simply your body's acknowledgement that something is not *currently* working—discomfort is not a sign that your success is never meant to be.

As you continue forward on your Alignment Journey, gift yourself permission to take comfort breaks, while inviting yourself *not* to shy away from discomfort. In both experiences, comfort and discomfort, consider what you are learning. As you create more space for inquiry, you will experience greater clarity—and the spiral continues on.

Clarity Practice Three: Follow Your Feelings and Go All In

Your third practice to foster clarity is to ask yourself: "then what?" or "what else?"

Follow your sensations—be it fear or excitement or confusion. Learn about your beliefs, values, assumptions, desires, and fears on a deep, experiential level.

Stay with your inquiry until a lightbulb goes off and you truly feel one aha moment of clarity.

UNDERSTAND THE POWER OF YOUR WORDS

Speaking intentionally has been one of the most profound shifts I've made with myself and my clients to increase self-awareness, question assumptions, and thus experience clarity. As a starting point, here are two profound (yet surprisingly simple) language shifts I invite you to adopt.

One of the easiest, quickest, and most life-changing shifts I make with clients is the incorporation of *I statements*.

In our English language, it is common to use *you* in place of I when talking about a personal matter. One might say, "You don't have to work out every day to be happy." When a more accurate statement would be "*I* don't have to work out every day to be happy." Another common example includes transforming a statement such as "You know when you have to run to catch the bus and feel so stressed the rest of the day?" to "When I have to run to catch the bus, I feel stressed the rest of the day."

As my clients consistently experience, there is power in this verbal transformation. I statements invite you to *own* your experience. They encourage personalization, rather than broad generalization: "I prefer" rather than "you prefer" or "we all prefer."

I statements also uncover powerful beliefs otherwise masked with the assumption that belief is truth. "You have to earn your spot at the table" is said without question, whereas "*I* have to earn my spot at the table" leaves room to ask yourself if this is true and desired by you.

I statements point to your values, your assumptions about yourself and others, and your preferences and requests. I statements provide the opportunity for your truth to be told and heard rather than figured out through passive language, fostering healthier relationships.

I statements change the game.

A second, transformational word shift is the phrase "historically speaking."

Sometimes, we speak about ourselves and our circumstances with bold claims, painting a picture not only of what has always been but manifesting what will always be.

For example, "I'm always late" may be a somewhat accurate statement for myself. It is also, however, an aspect of myself I have the ability to change. Historically speaking is a linguistic tool I can use to shift the paradigm.

Rather than stating "I am always late," I could choose to say: "Historically speaking, I'm always late." This shift provides just enough space to question whether the statement is still true and to ask myself, "Is this what I desire for my future?"

Here's another example: "He's not very nice" might feel true in your experience with an old coworker. But what if you haven't seen him in years? Could you provide space by saying, "Historically speaking, he wasn't very nice."

These scenarios do not necessitate change; it may be that I am still late or you still believe your coworker isn't very nice. However, adding in "historically speaking" provides *clarity* to re-decide—to see with fresh eyes—and, if it feels right, to begin again.

Historically speaking invites the possibility to shift. Historically speaking provides an opportunity to create your future with intention. Historically speaking reminds you that who you were yesterday needn't be who you are tomorrow. Historically speaking sets the foundation for evolution.

Clarity Practice Four:
Shift Your Word, Shift Your World

In my experience as a client and coach, it often takes an outside perspective to incorporate these powerful language shifts. Changing your language requires breaking patterns you've learned and adopted your entire lifetime—patterns which are often habitual and, thus, can be hard to hear on your own.

To pick up on your own speaking habits and adopt new speaking patterns that foster clarity, create a partnership with a trusted friend. Invite them to watch for your language patterns and introduce opportunities to try out linguistic shifts such as I statements and historically speaking.

To complete this practice on your own, try freewriting or recording yourself off the cuff. Tell a story about your day, or vent about a problem at work. Then, go back and highlight or note when you use the generalized *you* or make unnecessary broad statements that could shift into history.

Take note of what feels different when you use I statements and historically speaking. Notice the bits of clarity that follow simply changing your word, and intentionally add in these elements to create a new, more aligned reality.

Encouragement to Trust Your Clarity

Please. Do not dim your light. Your voice is the most beautiful thing I have ever heard.

It is not very loud—not yet—but when I close my eyes and ease into quiet breath, I hear absolutely: Your voice is humble and kind. It is remarkably intelligent. Its strength and courage translates through a grounded, bold tone—yet it chooses to whisper, for boisterous calls in the past have knocked you off your feet. Do not mistake its quiet volume for lack of fire.

Close your eyes, ease into quiet breath... Can you hear it, too?

Your voice is one of the most patient I have ever met. Allowing you to choose when to listen. Understand there are other elements at play: transformative growth, family hopes, rejection, life-changing success...

Your voice is there for you to listen, to use, to trust—now and twenty years from now. It will never go away, and there was never a time it did not exist.

Do not fall into patterns, believing you must work at this voice, or create it... Close your eyes, ease into quiet breath... It is already there. Can you hear it?

Your voice is one of the most important sounds I have ever heard. It has already changed lives. It has healed and celebrated. Your voice has offered mind-opening insight in offices and dining rooms alike. It has planted seeds you may never see flourish—while they undoubtedly do.

Your voice matters.

It is the point the universe is trying to make. It is the idea that will shift a generation, the love that will mend decades of loss. This is you, in the purest sense, thriving in this once-in-a-lifetime moment, thriving as our world craves its sound, its existence, its bold, remarkable, and quiet fire.

I can hear it.

Will you?

Your voice matters. Please hear it, trust it, scream it from your apartment window. Your voice matters. Your voice is your clarity.

Gain access to over eight additional practices for clarity by downloading your Alignment Journey workbook at yesandbymarin.com/workbook.

CHAPTER 5

Set Your Direction:
Admit Your Desire

So far on your Alignment Journey, you've followed your note of curiosity, instinct, or desire by exiting the river's flow... You created space on the riverbank to at last observe the world around you. After courageously letting in the light, you experienced clarity: clarity about your current experience, context about the beautiful landscape that surrounds you, insights about yourself you hadn't known to consider before...

Now, it hits you. Like the scene from a cartoon, where a boxing glove swings from the doorway above and stuns you into stillness.

"Oh sh!t. It's time to change."

Sometimes, this realization is terrifying. Sometimes, it's humorous. Sometimes, it feels striking or inspiring.

I call this the oh sh!t moment—the part of your Alignment Journey when you realize what you desire and dare to set your new direction.

This part of the Alignment Journey is an important step to differentiate, even if it seems to pass quicker than the other stages. Without distinction, you may dismiss oh sh!t insights as unsettling moments that knock you off your feet rather than powerful, directional guideposts that consistently lead you toward greater alignment. Furthermore, I encourage you to recognize this part of the journey, not only for how it begins but for the ripple effect that follows.

As an example, let's revisit my story from graduate school: I sat in a classroom with my PhD cohort. I asked a question to my favorite professor about how to prioritize a seemingly impossible workload. I was shocked at her answer—one that undoubtedly misaligned with my own values, desires, and well-being. At that moment, I realized the PhD program was not for me.

This oh sh!t moment in my Alignment Journey *felt* instantaneous—like a boxing glove to my forehead as I depicted earlier. In reality, this singular moment was the culmination of days, weeks, and months spent creating space and gaining clarity; already-gathered insights electrified together to prompt a moment of understanding.

My direction realization and accompanying oh sh!t continued as I stepped out of the PhD classroom like a deer in headlights. My world had turned upside down. The rug was pulled out from under me. My future felt scrambled.

In metaphor, instead of a gentle transition from space to clear vision to choosing the hiking trail I found in front of me, it felt like I was suddenly dropped in the middle of the forest with my space, clarity, and compass—but nothing else. The point is, I was shaken.

I felt further disoriented as I looked to the real mountains that bordered our graduate town. I looked at the same peaks as I had hours earlier, basked in the same heat I'd felt when I entered the classroom, and walked next to my same ambitious friends… The world around me was the same; what had changed was *me*.

I continued to experience oh sh!t moments as I developed an exit strategy from the program, built the courage to enact it, and considered the implication of my decision as I brainstormed a new career path and shared the news with advisors, family, and friends.

I'll talk more about the *recurrence* of oh sh!t moments later in this chapter. For now, think of a time you've experienced a similar circumstance: when one moment in time seemed to change everything.

My mentor, Coby Kozlowski, speaks to this as a "one degree revolution": one small shift can influence your entire life trajectory. Through metaphor, Coby tells the story of a boat on course toward a far-off destination. It may be impossible for a passenger on the ship or an observer from the shore to notice if the ship shifts one degree east—but if it does, the ship will eventually arrive in a far different place than its original course.

I imagine this step of the Alignment Journey as you, the captain of your own ship, shifting your gaze one degree east. You may not turn the wheel at this stage in the process—but your whole body will feel the changing winds, nonetheless.

Consider our river metaphor: you had once mindlessly floated down the stream or paddled like hell, then created space by resting on the riverbank. Next, you rubbed the water from your eyes to clearly see what existed around you. Oh sh!t arrives when you realize how much you love the idea of climbing the mountain you observe on the other side of the field.

Imagine it. You see what you desire. Your heart races at the thought of taking one step toward it, let alone climbing fourteen thousand feet. Sweat drops down your nose, and the hair on your neck stands up because you must admit returning to the river no longer feels right. Part of you might throw a tantrum and outline the perceived risks involved; this part of you begs to settle for *fine*, reminds you how warm the river water felt on your skin, and makes up stories about the scary monsters and steep terrain that resides on the mountainside.

But even as your breath quickens and eyebrows raise, your thought persists: "I'm about to climb that mountain." Welcome to the oh sh!t part of your journey.

The Benefit of Discomfort

Even as I explain this part of the journey in metaphor, my instinct is to run from this stage of the journey and avoid it at all costs. The oh sh!t feeling is freaking uncomfortable!

If you, too, sense yourself wanting to run when you encounter your world-flipping realization, congratulations! You are human. It is a natural instinct to run away from discomfort because in some instances avoiding discomfort keeps us alive. On the contrary, the type of discomfort you experience in the Alignment Journey is life-giving, rather than life-threatening.

We've been here before on the Alignment Journey. You're accustomed to discomfort as a beneficial and normal part of the journey from when you created space.

During the space and riverbank stage of your Alignment Journey, discomfort arose when you shifted from denial to truth-telling. Although scary, remaining open to discomfort in this stage enabled you to experience greater insights during your clarity and observation stage to follow.

In the current direction-setting stage of your Alignment Journey, discomfort will likely arise in the form of anticipation and self-doubt. Remaining open to discomfort while you admit your desire and direction will enable greater motivation for what is to come next: aligned action. Thus, just as you did before, trust the benefit of not only *accepting* discomfort but fully experiencing it.

Experiencing discomfort is your ultimate motivation to shift. If you've ever accidentally placed your hand on a hot stovetop, you know what I mean. In this physical example, you may even feel grateful for your discomfort—for if it didn't exist, you might have kept your hand on the hot surface for a dangerous amount of time, doing harm to yourself in the process. Because of pain and discomfort, you are triggered to let go, to move, and to learn.

What if the same gratitude you feel in response to quickly lifting your hand from the stovetop can be applied when you experience discomfort elsewhere—such as at work? What if, instead of avoiding work discomfort, you thanked it for prompting you to make a change—be it in the work itself, in your relationship to your job, or through a request with your manager? What if you felt grateful for work discomfort because it forced you to admit you're ready to pursue greater dreams?

Likewise, consider when you experience discomfort in your relationships. Can you imagine your discomfort as a useful indication that something needs to shift? Maybe your needs aren't being met, there's potential for growth, or you discover a necessary change to request from your partner or make personally.

In all instances, if you didn't experience discomfort in the first place, you wouldn't have a prompt to shift out of what isn't working.

To return to our metaphor, if you simply looked to the mountain after your bout of clarity but avoided any discomfort that accompanied actually leaving the river and climbing said mountain, you may reside in the comfortable space of looking at the mountain forever.

Take this to an extreme: imagine what you would do if you wanted to be as comfortable as possible while looking at this gorgeous mountain landscape. You might open up a lawn chair, add pillows and blankets to cozy in, and crack open your favorite drink as you admire the scene before you. Soon, your setup would not only make discomfort less appealing but ludicrous. Once you're under warm blankets, you would wonder why you would ever leave such a luxurious sanctuary for the treacherous mountainside. Plus, you can still see the mountain, right? "Good enough…"

Alternatively, imagine what you would do if you embraced discomfort. You would stare down your mountain, welcome in all the fears, and fully absorb the part of you that's wide awake to how ill-suiting the river was. You would gain more clarity as to why you are willing to pursue what you desire: because although the path forward is uncomfortable, where you came from promises even greater discomfort. Thus, you might feel surprised that right next to your fearful what-ifs exist joyful anticipation for what you will experience atop the mountain peak.

The discomfort of anticipation builds like bottled energy to project you toward your vision. Before you know it, you'll be on the mountainside thinking, "What did I get myself into?" and also "I will never look back."

Direction Practice One: Take Inventory of Past Oh Sh!t Moments

Journal, share with a friend, or call to mind three instances where you felt grateful for discomfort. When has discomfort been your guide? When would you have remained in an unhealthy or misaligned situation had it not been for discomfort?

Furthermore, what is your relationship with discomfort in oh sh!t moments, specifically? Remember one or two examples from your life when you've courageously declared a desire and set a direction that felt nerve-wracking, and undoubtedly aligned.

Part of Your Journey Forevermore (The Good News)

When she first reached out to me, one of my clients proclaimed her six-month goal was to determine whether or not to leave her current job. At the time, I had an instinct that she would far surpass this goal. Coaching collapses time, and just like the decision in front of you—if she was already questioning whether or not to leave her job, she already knew she wanted to leave her job.

During our first sessions together, we dove into her river to explore the underpinning of her experience: What, exactly, was feeling overwhelming at work? What factors led up to her burn out? What values were important to her and unmet in her current circumstance?

Once we found her riverbank and created space to ask these powerful questions, observations, and emotions—clarity ensued. She realized she was passionate about supporting others, but this passion had a shadow side, as well. Upon entering a career that helped disadvantaged individuals navigate extremely difficult situations, my client couldn't help but take on all of her client's struggles and frustrations as her own. She cared so much for others, she had forgotten to care for herself.

Shortly into our time together, we not only grasped what was misaligned about the river she had been floating in—we observed her greater landscape and pinpointed her mountain. She did, in fact, want to leave her job; her direction was set. Nonetheless, the same fears that kept her from admitting her desire at the start of our time together only multiplied when she considered taking action.

Sometimes, rather than a feeling, fear is a feisty contrarian: a voice with clever excuses as to why your set direction is wrong, unrealistic, and selfish. This last point, selfishness, was especially prominent for my client ready to leave her job.

As she looked to her mountain, she felt anxious about the conversations she knew stood at its base: sharing this decision with her partner and family, submitting her resignation with a beloved boss, and saying goodbye to coworkers and clients she enjoyed working with.

Furthermore, her stomach churned at the thought of how much uncertainty would follow her act of alignment. What would her next job be? How would she plan her finances without a guaranteed income stream? What will her new professional identity be?

Together, we held space for her fears, questions, and hesitations. Only after fully leaning into her discomfort was she confident enough to arrive at two consecutive oh sh!t moments: to officially set her direction to quit and to take action to follow through.

Although I've experienced many of these challenging moments with my clients, I was interested in the courageous, direction-setting moments that existed outside of a coaching relationship, as well. So while enjoying a cup of coffee on my family's pontoon at the lake, I explained what an oh sh!t moment felt like and asked if anyone had their own examples.

My brother's girlfriend shared the moment she realized it was time to move to Baltimore after accepting her admittance to Johns Hopkins. My mom shared the moment she understood that, before moving into her dream home, she would have to discard many of her current belongings, several of which held memories and meaning for her.

After listening intently to my family's examples, something new about this part of the Alignment Journey stood out to me: it seems we're surprised this stage of the journey repeats itself. It seems we assume things should eventually no longer feel daunting or scary, as if there comes a time when we've ventured this journey enough to no longer be swept off our feet with newfound insights and directions.

But that's the thing about oh sh!t moments: by definition, they're delightfully unexpected and consistently daunting.

Not only will you likely experience anticipation once you realize you want to climb your metaphorical mountain—you'll likely encounter anticipation after months of planning for your climb, when you realize it's time to strap in and climb. You'll likely experience another oh sh!t when you reach a challenging part of the mountain path and must recommit to your assent. Once you arrive at your original destination, create space for how incredible the view is and feel clarity about why that climb was so important for your particular journey… You may experience another bout of nerves when you feel called to jump on a mountain bike and ride back down the intimidatingly forest-covered, steep, and gorgeous mountainside—or feel just as challenged by an instinct to rest for months in the discovered mountain-top hammock.

Oh sh!t moments are a regular part of the Alignment Journey. They will not last forever, but they may temporarily knock you off your feet. If you lean into the discomfort, they will also provide abundant fuel to continue forward—and excitement about what lies ahead.

When an Oh Sh!t Moment Invites Pause

Earlier, I provided a stovetop metaphor for insightful oh sh!t moments—but a quick release isn't always the path you wish to take when you name a new direction. Sometimes, you may want to bask in your discomfort-filled moments. In my experience, this is especially true when your current Alignment Journey is coupled with grief.

Have you ever been in a sorrowful mood and intentionally turned on a sad playlist? Even if you had another option, such as to attend a friend's party or turn on your favorite sing-along, your preference may still be to cry alone in your room.

Alternatively, consider the unfortunate situation when you lose a loved one: what follows loss is an instinctual season of mourning. Sometimes, discomfort is the most comfortable feeling you can have. Thus, sometimes you may want to take pause instead of jump into action.

One of my most vivid examples of taking pause after realizing a deep-seated desire occurred during my final year of undergraduate studies.

On a surprisingly warm fall day, my mom and I took a walk alongside the lake a few miles from my university. She had been visiting from out of town, and I was updating her on my relationship—a topic that often made its way into our conversations during that season of my life.

Prior to this walk, many times, my mom had generously shared her patience, time, and space for me to work through the emotions, questions, and options I debated internally.

This time around, our conversation felt less about inquiry and more about neatly outlining my familiar story.

As the conversation neared its end, I felt my gaze rest on the large tree ahead of us. The path curved around it, avoiding the tree's deep roots that had kept it beside the water's edge for decades or centuries. As my eyes rested on the tree, I felt an unnerving conclusion rest in my mind, as well.

I sighed, "Oh sh!t," and my heart dropped. "I want to break up with him."

Whether I said this aloud or not, it felt palpable in the air. In a strange way, it also felt as if it had always been there—as if my mom had seen this clarity all along but allowed me to arrive in my own time. As if I had finally caught up to the truth.

The mud had settled, all questions had been asked and answered, multiple times, and I reiterated what I already knew to be true. "This is it…"

Admitting my desire felt more complex than desires and directions I'd set in the past. On one hand, my heart sank because my conclusion felt right. On the other hand, a large part of me still begged to pretend it was wrong.

I deeply cared for the person I was deciding to break up with. Even more, I felt love for him—something I assumed to be the only element needed to maintain a healthy and flourishing relationship.

My dispirited insight amplified because I knew I could not unsee my conclusion. The boxing glove had already hit my forehead. As I continued to walk lakeside with my mom, I knew my decision had been made.

So why did it take an entire year before this relationship officially reached its end?

Because a large part of me still fought for the alternative. Because I believed "if I just try a little harder, I can make this work." Because my beliefs needed time to change. Because the conclusion, in and of itself, brought grief along with it. Because there was another human, military service, a cross-country move, graduate school, and limited communication involved.

With a full list of justifications, I still felt guilty for not transitioning more quickly from the realization stage to the action stage of this particular Alignment Journey. Although I am still working through grief and remorse to this day, I offer myself compassion for doing my best at the time. I offer this same compassion to you.

If you are in the midst of an especially unnerving moment of direction and desire, please give yourself space to rest. Just because you've set your destination does not mean you must take immediate action. Gather extra assurance that you do, in fact, want to follow your desire. Give your fears and emotions time to be.

Of course, be compassionate and mindful of others' feelings, as well—and trust what is best for you is also best for them. Compassion will support you to navigate this stage with courage.

Remember, this is *your* journey. Pursue it in your own time, and in your own way. Opportunity to take action will be there when you're ready.

When an Oh Sh!t Moment Invites Action

If guilt or intentional pause is not present, a common belief that often hinders my clients from admitting to and pursuing their true desires is one of safety: "It would be safer to just stay where I am." A second common belief that hinders progress in this stage of the Alignment Journey centers around worthiness. My clients ask, outright or inadvertently, "Can't I just accept this life is good enough?" or "I should be grateful for what I have."

If you chose to abide by these beliefs, it'd likely look like the image we painted earlier of the comfortable lawn chair set up in front of your mountain view. And as stated then, this is an option for you to choose. I challenge you to at least consider, however, the assumptions under your limiting beliefs that arise during this stage of the journey—especially as you've already created space, experienced clarity, and set a direction based in grounded authenticity.

Regarding safety: Do you know, for certain, that your newfound direction is unsafe? Do you value safety more than following your heart's desire? Are you truly, for certain, safe if you remain exactly where you are?

Regarding worth: Does pursuing this desire necessarily imply you are not grateful for your current life? Are you being called toward greater abundance? If your friend shared a daring dream with you, would you say the same line: "Be grateful for what you already have"?

Again, lean into discomfort for what it's worth. For me, admitting *any* path is unsafe gave me permission to pursue the path of business ownership. For you, admitting you are grateful for your current life *and* desire more may enable you to take a vacation now instead of working eighty hours to prove your rest was earned.

When you hear and feel an oh sh!t insight land on your heart, your authenticity is telling you loud and clear there is a greater way for you to show up in this world. And if you do not listen this time, in my experience, your insight will only show up again and again, with increased force.

The part of you who tasted such great potential will undeniably proclaim, "This is important," "This is right for you," "Please listen, I am showing you the way." She will whisper it, and then scream it, until you follow suit. You may as well listen now.

Choose your truth. Choose to trust your journey thus far. The feeling that accompanies this stage of your journey is undeniable—and while at times you may welcome pause before taking action, pay close attention to what exists as you rest. If you are overcome with limiting beliefs and old storylines, tune back in to where your oh sh!t moment originated—with space, clarity, and true desire—and decide whether to sit in discomfort for motivation or leap forward toward action.

Direction Practice Two:
Differentiate When to Pause and When to Act

When you experience clarity about a direction or desire, do you tend to follow your guidance right away... or wait for extra assurance that it is the right direction to pursue? What is the outcome when you listen quickly versus wait for a few more knocks of insight?

Furthermore, start to differentiate the *types* of pause that exist between oh sh!t moments and proceeding action. Notice whether "I'll follow my instinct when I'm ready" is rooted in a place of trust, collaboration with the universe, and embracing your current emotions and experiences. Alternatively, notice whether your pause stems from avoidance, limiting beliefs, or denial.

List two examples when you have experienced each type of pause. When have you paused due to trust and self-compassion? When have you paused due to fear and excuses? Then, how can you differentiate these pauses to better inform your future oh sh!t moments?

Enjoy Your Anticipation Before You Climb

Recently, my life coach and I created a new perspective of the oh sh!t stage by considering how it feels to stand at a mountain trailhead. Remember the caricature exercise? I invite you to parallel the story I'm about to share by dramatizing *your* most prevalent internal voices as unique characters. In turn, you will gain greater insight and understanding of your motivations and barriers during this part of the Alignment Journey.

With my coach, I anticipated new business growth ahead (oh sh!t). To organize my thoughts, we separated emotions, thoughts, and worries into caricatures—including a hiker, a mountain ranger, a guide, and my future self. Soon, a clarifying story emerged.

All four characters prepared to begin our mountain hike toward our next business venture. My hiker seemed nonchalant as she checked supplies and buckled on her backpack. She wore cute, relaxed clothing and listened to today's top hits through her headphones. Although she felt anticipation for our climb to the mountain's peak, it was balanced with excitement.

My ranger, in her brown girl scout uniform complete with twenty badges, clutched her clipboard with white knuckles. She felt hesitant to get on the trail without reading the safety checklist at least three more times. She commanded everyone else to memorize the rules, as well. "Ensure this much money stays in our bank account at all times." "We cannot let ourselves overwork." "Beware of sneaky traps set by competition and internet trolls!"

My mountain guide stood a few feet ahead of the rest, with eyes glued on the trail map posted at the entrance. She wore a hat and backpack full of every tool we should need. She was proud that we'd chosen to take a new path and seemed well-prepared, though she incessantly recalculated mileage and laid out worst-case scenarios.

Then, there was my future self. My future self stood tall with confidence and ease a few steps beside us. She'd already climbed this mountain several times, and she made sure we knew it. She had a blast as she joked with the rest of us about wild animals and getting lost in the wilderness. She rolled with giddy laughter as everyone else shrieked with fright.

Before building out this scene with my coach, I felt scared in anticipation of my uncertain business trajectory;

although clear and desired, my newfound direction felt sporadic and overwhelming. Now, I understood why: multiple parts of me were trying to prioritize their needs simultaneously, without avail.

Through this session, I developed a way to organize and relate with my main characters (aka, my thoughts, desires, and fears) in that moment and for future moments of anticipation.

If my hiker feels overwhelmed, I can speak to her with compassion: "You're doing great, keep up the good work! Thank you for following directions so nicely. An entire team is taking care of you."

If my ranger starts to panic, I can give her space to calm down: "Thank you for reminding me to check my bank account. We're all good! Yes, taxes are accounted for. Yes, we have enough money to make this big investment. I know you want us to be safe—I promise, we are safe."

If my guide is spinning in circles, I can give her busy work or grant her permission to rest: "Good news, you get a vacation! I'll call you once we're done with this ride, or halfway through, so we can start planning what's next. Right now, we're all set—thank you for getting us here!"

Lastly, I trust there is part of me that knows the future. Especially in uncertain times, I can lean on her to ask: "What do you see that I can't?" Furthermore, I can laugh with her, "Thank you for reminding me to chill out and have fun."

As is possible for you, I now feel in control of how to navigate moments of overcoming anticipation by hearing my various needs and speaking to myself with intention.

Even better, just as I've experienced as I prepare for a grand adventure in real life, I can now explore *joy* in these challenging moments.

As you navigate this stage of the Alignment Journey, invite yourself to feel anticipation like giddy excitement at the base of a trailhead. Or if hiking isn't your jam, consider the moments leading up to a roller coaster ride. Excitedly anticipate the thrill that follows preparation. Feel a smile lift the corners of your mouth, take a breath, and allow yourself to laugh as your future self jokes about what is to come.

Because next comes action. Next, all parts of you will start their climb up the hill and discover opportunities you don't yet know exist. The energy that builds up during this stage will fully release because whatever you are worried about at this moment pales in comparison to the wonders and sights you are about to experience.

Action comes next. Now, and only now, is your opportunity to experience the before… the anticipation… the oh sh!t. Just like at the base of a mountain, or the forefront of any wild adventure, lean into your anticipation stage with joy. "Here. We. GO!!"

Gain access to over seven additional practices to navigate the oh sh!t stage by downloading your Alignment Journey workbook at yesandbymarin.com/workbook.

CHAPTER 6

Start Walking:
Take Aligned Action

For years, I dreamt of adopting a puppy.

...and when I say "dreamt of," I mean I purchased dog treats, I posted a Think Pawsitive sign in my office, and I scheduled "walk dog" in my calendar. I am not joking; I walked an imaginary dog every day for months to proactively build the routine into my schedule. Although one important aspect of this task was missing (the dog), I spent each minute of these walks manifesting my someday reality.

Years after implementing manifestation and mindset practices to prepare for my dog, I hosted a retreat for my coaching clients that included a vision board exercise. After completing the practice, my clients shared boards covered in images that depicted their greatest dreams and passions. Then, I shared my own.

As I pointed to a picture of a yellow Labrador, I was surprised to experience an emotion akin to annoyance. "Why is this still an image on my vision board?" I internalized. I'd talked about getting a dog for ages; a puppy had been on the last four vision boards I'd created. Instead of dreamy, the dog image felt redundant.

Mindset, belief, and preparation are essential steps to realize grand dreams. I do not discredit their utility, just as I do not discredit the first three stages of the Alignment Journey—but they are only three of seven stages in the Alignment Journey. With my dream dog, I had been creating space, fostering clarity, and setting my dog-mom direction for years.

It turns out the perfect rescue puppy, soon to be named Aatto, was already waiting for me. Furthermore, I had already created the lifestyle, habits, and mindset to adopt him with ease. There was only one missing link: action. The final step to ensure my vision came to life was emailing Happy Tails Rescue, driving to a meet and greet, and submitting payment for my furry companion.

As I type this, Aatto's little paws rest on the floor next to my desk. I own a dog—a dog I adopted the same week I shared my fourth puppy vision board with my clients. I shake my head and smile at how easy it was to bridge the gap between desire and reality. Likewise, I wonder how many dreams are waiting to be realized by you with one small action.

What if your dream is right in front of you? What if your final step is to act?

Many of my clients ask how to balance manifestation, trust in the universe, and showing up to take action for what is right in front of us. To this, I say: "Yes, and…"

Yes: dream, paint vision boards, and share your desires with dear friends. And: open your eyes to your role in creating the dream.

Yes: trust the universe and know there are infinite possibilities for how your dreams will unfold. And: remember you, too, are the universe. You, too, hold capability and possibility to actualize what you desire.

Stop Preparing for Your Journey

Already on your Alignment Journey, you have courageously left your passive river, found your riverbank to create space, observed your surroundings to experience clarity, and set your sights on the mountain you desire to determine aligned direction (oh sh!t!).

All along, you've been preparing to step into this moment of the journey with confidence; you've metaphorically or literally packed your bags, drawn a map, set a timeline, and taken a few breaths to build confidence in yourself and in your forthcoming venture.

You are prepared to take action, already.

But just like other aspects of the Alignment Journey, action presents its own discomfort and fear. Especially if you are a perfectionist, you may feel more comfortable in the steps already completed—the steps of preparation. Thus, your comfort zone may entice you to revert back to a previous step of the Alignment Journey instead of continuing toward unpredictable action.

Likely, if you pause or step backward at this point in the journey, it is not because more space, clarity, and direction are needed—it is because preparation feels safe and known.

You are already prepared. You have already packed, planned, and organized yourself enough. Trust this, so you can create your dreams rather than endlessly prepare for their arrival.

Like my client who spoke about her dream to organize a cooking course during one of our first sessions together—and then took action. Within two months of working together, she had a fully outlined course and earned $1,300 after her first launch.

Like my client who mentioned wanting to move his business completely online during our first consultation—and then took action. During our first coaching session together, he celebrated closing an unfulfilling and outdated workspace.

Like my client who expressed stress and burnout from her job—and then took action. We celebrated together just three months into coaching when she submitted her long overdue resignation with confidence and clarity.

Like my client who brainstormed a new role in her company—and then took action.

Like my client who realized she was her best self when traveling—and then took action.

Like my client who knew it was time to increase her service prices—and then took action.

One Stepping-Stone at a Time

"What should I do first?" is a question I hear from many clients during the action stage of their Alignment Journey. When my clients ask this question, they often feel overwhelmed and scattered and lack the confidence to make any decision, let alone lay out a full action plan to fulfil their dream. Maybe you feel the same.

What often accompanies feelings of paralyzing overwhelm is a belief that there are only a few significant actions to take. The reality is you take action every minute of every day—so frequently, in fact, that our brain has to put some actions on autopilot such as breathing, navigating our route to work, and recognizing faces.

The aligned action you take today is not the only action you will ever make. So take your best guess. Decide. And act.

The most important part of this stage in your Alignment Journey is to do something, no matter how small; it is to move the needle even a millimeter toward greater alignment. So find a path that's approachable and do it.

I encourage you to consider the action stage of your Alignment Journey not as one big move but many small steps. Rather than continuously circling back to one "should I or shouldn't I" action such as "Do I quit my job?," break your action steps into something more manageable. Try, instead, "Do I want to start browsing job boards?" or "Will I tell my partner I'm discontent at work?" Small decisions and bite-size actions reduce overwhelm and invite opportunity to celebrate along the way.

A stepwise approach preserves significant energy and resources as you quickly experience whether your choice fosters or detracts from your best life. Every small action step you take enlists a sense of accomplishment, a feedback loop to determine your progress, and the opportunity to better align with your ultimate goal: Is this action serving the purpose I assumed it would? Is this action stepping me closer to my intended outcome?

As a bonus, small actions also allow you to embrace the goodness that already exists on your journey, rather than incorrectly assume you cannot be happy, satisfied, or successful until total alignment is achieved.

Consider how a hiker summits a mountain through incremental steps. To start, they've likely hiked many times before this specific climb. Through their own version of space and clarity, they set their eyes on a desirable mountain peak and determined it as their new direction. Of course, the hike itself is accomplished by stepping one foot after the other—gripping one rock and then another. But even before this, they chose a training regimen, learned the advanced skills needed for this particular terrain, spoke with experts who have navigated the area before, and enlisted support from fellow climbers. They chose what tools to bring with them, loaded their packs, and drove to the trailhead. They triple-checked the weather, their map, and their backpack of survival tools. Then, they stepped onto the path and continued forward one footprint at a time.

The action for a climber is not to summit the mountain. Action is every step along the way. Small, outlined, and accountable action steps are key to a hiker's success—and the same small-step approach is true for your journey's success.

How to Determine Your Pace

If your oh sh!t, desired-direction mountain was to embody self-confidence, what would aligned action look like? A big action step might be to adopt the belief, "I am absolutely confident in every decision I make" or even, "I am confident in myself."

While this may be your ultimate desire, in my experience a shift this great can feel overwhelming and fire up paralyzing, unhelpful fear and resistance. Like a first-time climber tackling Mount Everest, the result of unnecessarily bold action leads to failure—failure to summit or failure to embody self-confidence at all.

Small action is all about pursuing what you are willing and able to tackle in the present moment. Rather than shifting from "I don't trust myself" to "I am confident in myself," a small, aligned action would be to adopt the belief, "I am capable of trusting myself."

This new belief still walks you closer to your ultimate goal of self-confidence without unrealistic expectations or unnecessary frustration. By taking accessible, aligned action, you not only act where you otherwise may have fallen short or succumbed to self-doubt—you start to create a new pattern. You gather evidence to grow stronger in yourself and in your beliefs. Then, you take more aligned action.

You buy what orange juice you desire at the grocery store because you trust your instincts. You stand from your desk to take a break from the workday because you trust your physical body. You lie down to rest early because you trust your sleepy eyes.

In time, small, aligned action steps build upon each other. Soon, you will arrive at your mountain summit and realize you are living in alignment with your ultimate belief, undoubtedly and completely: "I am confident in myself."

Likewise, when my client from chapter four approached me with a mountain desire to quit her job, I did not start session one with "Okay. So how will you quit?" Once we created space, experienced clarity, and officially set her confident direction to quit, we started with brave yet approachable action.

We brainstormed a list of ways she could take one small step out of misalignment, and one step into greater alignment. She chose one item to enact at a time, without pressure for it being the best, right one—because there were many more to come.

While the big goal to quit her job remained the centerpiece for our work together, we used a small-step approach. In turn, each step was accompanied with the opportunity to strengthen her trust in herself and in the Alignment Journey, learn what true alignment felt like, and incorporate a plan that not only helped her step away from misalignment but prepare for a more aligned future.

During this stage of your Alignment Journey, remember to start small and stay specific, like an Everest climber in training. Small, aligned action fosters your possibility to celebrate small victories and see evidence of exciting progress, to make informed decisions with new information, adjust your sails, and take continuous, sustainable action. Approached in this way, action will empower you to continue your pursuit of big alignment goals without fearing overwhelm in your journey.

Return to your oh sh!t moment and desired direction. What aligned steps would move you toward your desired destination by one inch? How could you make it even more simple, and what small, aligned action will you take today?

Action Practice One: Dream Big, Step Small

To build trust in and experience the benefit of approachable, aligned action, turn to your physical body. Sit on a flat surface with your legs extended in front of you. Take a deep breath, extend your spine tall, and slowly walk your fingers alongside your legs. As your heart shines toward your toes, take note of your breath.

If you feel a deep stretch and maintain calm breath, you've found your sweet spot for small, aligned action. If you reach beyond your body's limit and your breath tightens or disappears, take a step back.

When you push yourself too far in this exercise, your breath and body tense, meaning although you may exert more effort, you no longer make true progress toward your goal. During my years as a yoga teacher, a large part of my job was to remind students of this: to breathe and relax, to find their sweet spot.

Instead of forcing bold unnecessary action, thereby inducing your reactionary fight, flight, or freeze response, trust the attractive, still progressive step in front of you. As you will experience in this stretching exercise, opting for action within your ability always reaps greater benefit than trying to force something you aren't ready for.

After this exercise, continue to use your breath to determine your pace in all pursuits. If you ever feel you cannot breathe (metaphorically or literally), this is your cue to step smaller.

Differentiate Real Fear from an Overzealous Ranger

Even if you break down your clarified direction into small, aligned action steps, fear may appear during the action stage of your Alignment Journey. When fear arises, it is not always a sign you are on the wrong path. In fact, upward energy fear may be better explained as excitement. To determine whether your fear is something to listen to or move on from, check in with where your fear is coming from and what your fear feels like.

In my experience as a coach and human navigating my own fears, the type of fear that is advantageous for us to listen to is obvious. This is the same fear that arises in a dark alleyway—the one that clearly tells you: "something is wrong"—and prompts you to get out of a bad situation.

If that is not how you explain the fear you feel at this stage of your journey, my best guess is you're experiencing a bunch of BS.

Advantageous fear originates from a place of truth, trust, and higher-self energy. At the thought of true fear and misaligned action, your chest feels concave, your shoulders roll forward, and your emotions portray an unsettling "oh no." If these descriptions feel true to you, revisit our yoga analogy: Might there be a smaller decision or action that feels more approachable? You may wish to return to stage one of the Alignment Journey and create space to explore your fear.

Alternatively, BS fear is rooted in unfounded storylines, self-doubt, and ego. At the thought of aligned, though scary, action, your eyebrows may lift, you may bite your lip in nervous anticipation, and your emotions portray an exciting "oh boy!" Maybe you're afraid about the unknown, or you question your worth to pursue something great. Regardless, this type of fear does not indicate life-threatening action—this type of fear indicates new.

This second type of fear is simply your desire for security, comfort, and familiarity. Your internal mountain ranger (picture my girl scout badge, clipboard-loving ranger I shared in chapter three) doesn't want you to take action because an upleveled life on the mountain peak is unknown, and unknown is scary. Accordingly, this fear may craft boisterous stories, illegitimate worries, and what-if scenarios that often succeed in at least prompting hesitation.

While the first type of fear elicits a beneficial reroute, you may release the second type of fear through acceptance and curiosity. Once you do so, return to your approachable, aligned action plan and move forward.

Take Action Now

As you are familiar by now, my graduate education included tireless work. Alongside my peers, I struggled to meet seemingly impossible deadlines, complete reading lists, study for exams, and make strides through independent research.

In the midst of all of this, I was surprised to hear an internal whisper that suggested I take voice lessons.

I was already a few months into teaching myself guitar—and I'd experienced the positive effect this had on my life. Guitar became my creative outlet in the midst of intellect overload. Guitar transformed a breakup of grief into one of poetry. Guitar had become my meditation—wherein I lost track of time, worry, and conflict even when tough classes and a full workload waited for me on the other side.

Maybe the thought of voice lessons shouldn't have come as a surprise. Nonetheless, it felt ridiculous to add an hour commitment into my already-packed schedule—let alone an hour commitment toward something nonessential.

I questioned taking action for weeks after the thought initially entered my mind. I came up with excuses, including that I had no intention to become a professional singer nor did I need to sing along with my guitar.

Yet, my desire to take voice lessons remained. One day, I thought, "What if desire is enough?"

I made the decision to at least inquire about voice lessons (i.e., I took small, aligned action). I sent three email requests to nearby music schools, and one replied with an excited invitation to take my first lesson free of charge.

I took a breath, checked in with my aligned foundation of space, clarity, and direction, and said yes.

I attended voice lessons every Friday at 2 p.m. throughout my last year of graduate school. Each week presented a new deadline, another excuse, stress, and pressure to prioritize academic work instead. My advisors insisted I didn't have time. My mountain ranger pointed to my calendar and suggested voice lessons did not belong.

Yet I continued to show up. I continued to prioritize life outside of stress and work. I continued to trust in doing something simply because I enjoyed it.

In hindsight, this choice and dedication to experience life through voice lessons—especially when I could reel off a list of reasons why I did not have permission—changed my life. My commitment to voice lessons was not only a commitment to joy but a commitment to my core values and to my authentic self.

What this required of me was action. Action to inquire, action to show up, and action to defend myself from misaligned beliefs and lifestyle choices. Furthermore, it required I surrender my list of excuses, as well as the excuses provided by those around me, to uphold my greater alignment.

I introduced "maybe in my next life" at the very beginning of this book. Return to this thought to motivate your action now; call out your assumption about what would be different after [fill in the blank]—after you earn more money, turn a certain age, finish your degree, find your life partner, or have x number of clients.

Not only do we prevent action by making blanket statements like "maybe someday," we also fool ourself about how much we change from one milestone to the next.

You are already capable and enough, by all definitions of the word, to do what you're called to do. Who you are today is not so different from who you were yesterday—which is also to say, who you will be in five years is also not so different from who you are today.

This is great news. This means you already know pretty darn well what will work and what will not work to motivate you toward your desired direction. Use who you know yourself to be today to make genuine change rather than rely on a magical date or milestone to dictate your action and results.

Action Practice Two: Build Courage to Take Action

Take a moment to outline any fears and excuses that accompany your present action step.

To start, is your fear a true indication of misalignment, or does it feel unfounded and limiting? Are your listed excuses worthy of outweighing your aligned action step and desired mountain?

Next, consider a time you've taken a risk in the past: What fears and excuses did you have leading up to this action? How did you feel about these fears and excuses once you took action?

Finally, get curious about what you think would be different in your "next" life. Could it be you have everything you need right now?

With your arsenal of action motivation, ask honestly: Will you choose your fears and excuses or your greatest alignment? If you are ready, take a big breath and act. Yes—right now. And if you're not ready, continue reading and look forward to action soon.

Trust in Your Journey Thus Far

I've introduced various storylines from my personal Alignment Journeys throughout this book—including leaving my PhD program, quitting work to pursue my coaching business, and realizing misalignment in a former relationship. This is what honest, aligned action looked like in each scenario:

I stared out my window in Claremont, California and looked at the desert mountains. Silence fell between my coach and me. I had exhausted my list of excuses to stay where I was in a misaligned graduate school program. I had given ample space, understood myself and my circumstance, and was facing a direction that felt terrifying and right.

I sighed the air from my strained chest out my nose. After a long breath of surrender, I closed my eyes. My coach didn't need any more information than that—we both knew what action was next.

I was about to change my status from PhD candidate to master's student, and no one around me was going to like it.

* * *

I entered the negotiation call with an open mind, hoping my boss and I could find a middle ground that felt great for us both. A half hour in, however, I knew my nonnegotiables were not met.

A seemingly large part of me wanted to fold my hand and agree with her offer. This was the only substantial income I had at the time, and I believed multiple stories about why this experience would benefit my career. Certainly, I was scared.

But I had made a promise to myself—and more powerful than my fear was my trust. I trusted my longing for more. I trusted my ability to support myself in a different way. I trusted my coaching business's ability to thrive.

"I believe it would be best for all involved if I concluded working on this project," I declared aloud, sweat forming on my forehead. My now-former boss was agreeable and nondramatic. We hung up the phone.

Immediately, I lay face-down on my office floor. I didn't know how else to cope with the fears that flooded my mind: "Why can't you just be grateful with the opportunities you have! Why do you make everything so difficult! How are you going to make money?! You've burned a bridge!"

They were loud, but what felt more certain was the voice in my heart that boldly whispered, "Yes. Trust me. Trust yourself. You will be okay."

*   *   *

My phone rang one evening from an unknown number. I knew who it was immediately; this is how calls arrived from the military ship my then-boyfriend was stationed on.

A year earlier, I walked lakeside with my mom and concluded the relationship was misaligned (oh sh!t). At the time, however, the part of me that suggested it could still be mended, worked through, and resolved wasn't ready to let go.

We tried, and I felt grateful for that. My partner and I adjusted, compromised, and remained curious as we entered a new stage of our lives together. Nonetheless, I could never shake that deep knowing within me, and it was time.

"I need to tell you…" I can't remember the words I used to end our relationship on the phone that day, but I remember his reply exactly: "I'm proud of you." My mind tried to understand what he meant until he added, "I want to fight for you, but it sounds like you've made up your mind."

For a long time, I reflected back on this moment. Could he have changed my mind? Could we have found resolve? Would I have avoided endless therapy sessions, sadness, and confusion that filled the years to follow?

Yet when I returned to that moment in time, I also knew he was right. I had made up my mind; I had spent months and years making up my mind—to be certain about taking action on something that would change our lives so significantly.

In brave, scary moments of action, this is what you have to hold onto: Trust in your journey thus far. Trust in the roots of your actions. Trust you have already created space, experienced clarity, and set a direction in alignment with your best self. In turn, you have taken action in alignment with what is best for everyone else.

Actions of alignment can feel especially powerful, scary, and new. I contend, in fact, actions of alignment will stand out above the rest because they are necessarily unique from any other action you or anyone else has taken before. By design, these actions do not follow the rulebook adopted by others—because actions of alignment come from within you, a place no one else has ever been.

This type of new, authentic action requires bold courage. Bold courage comes from a place of internal groundedness—the only foundation that cannot be shaken or taken from you. In moments when you feel strong and courageous, take a few slow, deep breaths to savor it. Or capture certainty in yourself with a visual: wear a bracelet, paint a picture, or set your running shoes by the door.

If doubt arises in the face of action, return to the emotions you intentionally experienced earlier in your Alignment Journey: the excitement and certainty associated with where you're going and what you desire, and the dissonance you never want to experience again. Bring into focus your clear direction. Take a few more deep breaths.

Always: Trust you have done enough. Trust your deep knowing, already delineated. Lean on your support systems and accountability. And *act*. Act with full knowing that this is the best guess you have at this time—and you are capable not only of enacting the step in front of you but managing whatever follows it.

Then, trust some more.

Action Practice Three: Just Do It

In one area of your life, you have already created space, experienced clarity, and set a direction. It's time to act.

What makes this action different from any other you've taken is that you've already completed steps one through three of the Alignment Journey; this action no longer stems from a place of obligation, an external opinion, or a misaligned rule book. This action originates from what you know to be best for you.

So take a big breath, and do the thing: Walk to your boss's office to submit your termination. Book your flight to visit the mom you never met. Send your payment to officially begin working with a new coach. Tell your partner what you were always too timid to share.

If you need an extra boost of confidence, consider what motivates you: a list, an accountability buddy, a reward, or a deadline. Set this for yourself, and then commit to follow through.

If you'd like some laughter to accompany this practice, search online for "Shia LaBeouf Just Do It." Trust me, it's hilarious and will become your go-to skit when action feels hard.

Gain access to the most important action practice by downloading your Alignment Journey workbook at yesandbymarin.com/workbook.

Or, take the shortcut and visit yesandbymarin.com/experience. Joining the Yes& community may be the most important action you take for a sustainable, supported, and fun Alignment Journey.

CHAPTER 7

Embrace Your Switchbacks: Trust the Ride

Congratulations! You have created space for clarity, set an aligned direction for your authentic future, and taken one action step toward your ideal reality. At this point in your Alignment Journey, you may experience relief, joy, and celebration. On the contrary, what follows action in the Alignment Journey can also feel much more nuanced.

When you take action toward something, even if that something excites every ounce of your soul, you inevitably take action away from something else. Because of this, in addition to or in replacement of relief, joy, and celebration, you may experience grief at this stage of the Alignment Journey.

At the very least, you may grieve comfort and a level of knowing that felt easy—even if what used to be was misaligned. You may have also stepped away from something that was *not* obviously misaligned to step toward something of greater alignment. Thus, there may be times when you grieve something you deeply cherished.

You may have stepped away from beloved parts of who you were: an identity, connection, or way of being that was joyous in its own right. To pursue alignment, you may have also stepped away from something you love: a lifestyle, community, or intimate partner.

This nuance compounds together to create your current stage of the Alignment Journey: the ride.

I originally heard this phrase from my coach, Coby Kozlowski, who speaks to riding the waves of life in her book, *One Degree Revolution*. During one of my retreats with her, she encouraged us to surf the ocean and physically experience what it means to embrace our inevitable ups and downs.

In the Alignment Journey, I use the ride to represent the vast waves of emotion that follow aligned action, no matter how right the action was or how confident you are in your aligned direction. In relation to our river metaphor, the ride is akin to switchbacks on your mountain, which lead you toward your destination though may not always feel like a direct path.

A Lookout Worth the Heartbreak

With a towel wrapped loosely around my chest, I stared blankly at the dresser on the other side of my rented room. My forehead burned, and my cheeks were stained with dry tears.

Had I made the right choice?

It had been months since our final phone call, yet I still felt conflicted and overwhelmingly sad with regard to the end of our relationship. Had I broken it off at the right time, in the right way? If heartbreak was the inevitable outcome, why did it need to begin in the first place? How could I have been so certain we were destined for forever?

"I'm not sure" and "It was my best guess" were the only answers I could summon at the moment. I closed my eyes and placed both hands on my chest. I invited myself to stay curious about what I felt. Is this sadness? Is this heartache?

The image that came to my mind was a deep red heart. Slowly, a gorgeous but harrowing gold line zigzagged up the middle and split the heart in half. The visual was overcoming—I fell sideways onto my bed and continued the sobs that began in my candlelit bathtub hours earlier.

This pattern of deep grief would continue for years. At moments, my grief felt unnecessarily dramatic—like when I curled in a fetal position on my bed that afternoon. Yet it was my true experience for a long time.

I transitioned through anger and denial to hope and curiosity about my new future. I felt both free and trusting—while simultaneously experiencing the worst heartbreak I had ever navigated. And it all came back to me: I had ended the relationship. I had chosen the grief of separation over the dissonance of staying in misalignment.

Amid grief and question, I remained steadfast in my decision because I had built my strong foundation; I had created space, experienced clarity, set my direction, and rested as my oh sh!t moment settled. I had done all of this before taking action.

Still, I ached for reassurance at times. I wanted some sort of proof that this ride was worth it—for both myself and my ex-partner. On my bed that afternoon, the only proof I had was my intuition there was something better. It felt ridiculously intangible.

A year later, in the spring of 2018, I graduated with my master's degree. Thereafter, I traveled 2,713 miles from California to the Midwest with my carload of possessions. A good friend accepted my invitation to join me on the adventure, and we looked forward to visiting every national park along the way. On the top of our list was Yosemite.

Both of us had heard Yosemite was one of the most beautiful places on earth. Friends described their visits as awe-inspiring and had shared photos with me to fortify what they meant. Their images captured the sunrise on El Capitán, expansive redwood forests, and rushing waterfalls over stunning rock. Thus, I already knew about the beauty of Yosemite. Upon our arrival, however, I quickly learned there is a difference between knowledge and experience.

As my friend and I stood on an overlook a few hours into our hike, I could hardly comprehend the gorgeous valley and sun-stained cliffs of Yosemite. Although I had anticipated this moment, nothing compared to the real-time experience of having my breath swept away.

Then—while standing on this cliff overlooking the vast, impressive landscape of Yosemite—it clicked.

My friends had promised a magnificent Yosemite experience, and I had seen pictures to prove it. Yet, there I was, looking at the exact same image with surprising awe and wonder. Correspondingly, my intuition had promised a magnificent, aligned relationship, but at times I doubted its reality.

Although seemingly unrelated, as I stood cliffside at Yosemite, my doubt vanished. I set the intention to trust my future relationship would be greater than any image my mind could conjure today—and I trusted the ride would be worth it.

AFTER LETTING GO: TRUST, TRUST, AND TRUST AGAIN

It is not just about taking aligned action. It is not just about letting go.

That decision in and of itself is likely difficult: To let go. To open your palm and choose to release something you once treasured. To invite something else into your life—an aligned vision not completely formed or realized, something exciting or a bit scary… something that may exist in your present moment only in the form of hope.

To take action and let go is a courageous, powerful act.

And it is not just about letting go.

It is also about breathing deeply in the midst of somber tears, holding your heart as it aches—moments or years after your release. It is also about trusting, and trusting, and trusting that your intuition was correct and your hope is true.

It is existing in a space of simultaneousness: to love and to have loved, to understand and disagree, to see what could be and choose otherwise.

It is holding compassion for the old version of yourself that thought for certain something else was the answer. It is embracing confusion and ambiguity when you do not know for certain any answers, anymore. It is seeing, even vaguely, your beautiful path proceeding.

Taking action is one step of your journey, which may include letting go. Be compassionate with yourself. Trust. (Trust.) And reach for support when you need it.

You are doing the best you can, with the information you have. Believe in what is coming; believe in what will be.

A Mountain Path Is Never a Straight Line

I use the end of my relationship to illustrate the ride because breakups are one of the most palpable versions of this stage in the Alignment Journey. Of course, the ride is not reserved solely for breakups.

I experience the ride to this day as I build my coaching business and navigate the excitement and uncertainty of entrepreneurism. My clients experience the ride as they pursue new endeavors, ask for promotions at work, go on dates for the first time since their divorce, and move countries—among so many other examples.

The ride is a part of this journey because alignment invites you to actively step away from what is familiar and step into something new. No matter what your new experience is, you will inevitably be met with surprise, emotional turbulence, and unanswered questions, simply because you have never been here before.

I've witnessed many individuals panic once they enter the ride. After one unexpected switchback, I hear my clients worry if they've made a bad choice, taken a wrong turn, or chased the wrong dream.

Of course, when questions like this arise, you can always return to step one of the Alignment Journey. Create space for everything that comes up—and in this space, you may have a new insight or greater clarity. In turn, you may even choose to slightly shift your direction and thus take a different action step.

However, I caution you from doing this simply due to a worry that surprises, or a full experience of emotions, indicate something is wrong; the ride is an inevitable part of the journey.

It may feel easier to accept the Alignment Journey as a linear roadmap from misalignment to celebrated, authentic success. I won't eliminate this as a possibility; maybe a linear Alignment Journey occurs for some people. In my experience, however—and what I want to prepare you for—is a journey that looks more like a hiking path through the mountains.

Consider the Alignment Journey, and this stage in particular, as one that zigzags back and forth and includes miles that seem to go backward. Even backward miles make sense once you realize they serve a purpose: to avoid a rockslide or a scary passage that flirts with a treacherous edge.

To illustrate this point further, I invite you to return to our river metaphor. So far in the Alignment Journey, you've stepped out from the water, cleared your eyes to observe what surrounds you, selected your mountain destination, and packed your bags to step toward it. After pausing, because "oh sh!t, I'm about to do this," you started to climb.

Now, in the ride, you take in your first moments on the trail. You notice the beauty of moss-covered trees. You meet new friends who hike the same path as you. Your view is breathtaking—literally, you may be out of breath. "How are we only an hour in?!" Then, you realize you forgot a crucial item and panic—until you brainstorm a solution.

You grow tired and experience the pain of blistered feet. You second-guess why you're climbing this mountain in the first place—in hindsight, that river was pretty great. You take a breath in the shade, get a hit of energy, and continue on with a smile on your face and trust in your heart.

At last, you come upon an overlook. From this vantage point, you can see for miles and catch a view of the river where you started. Deep gratitude and pride fall over your tired body. You walk a bit further to your gorgeous campsite for the night and bask in a newfound sense of freedom, health, and trust in your climb.

Then, you befriend a talking bear.

Okay... so maybe you do not befriend a bear—but just as that turn of events may have made you laugh, sometimes your Alignment Journey is so unpredictable and surprising that you cannot help but laugh it off.

The Alignment Journey promises the most beautiful life I could ever imagine—but this does not mean it comes without challenge. The Alignment Journey includes a full variety of hardship that you must navigate, process, and relate with if you want to reach your true and most full potential.

Even after moving in with a wonderful man—indeed, the Yosemite relationship I held trust in for years—loss, confusion, and heartache still visit every now and again. Most recently, I unexpectedly found the letters my ex and I had exchanged during his months of military boot camp. I was reminded not only of him, but of the future I had planned with him. I dropped my head into my hands over my kitchen table and sobbed. My deep emotions felt familiar, and I was transported back to that moment years ago on my bed only days after our breakup.

I could have mislabeled my recent sobs as a sign that I had made the wrong choice. Fortunately, I have my strong and true foundation to lean upon (the foundation you created, as well, if you fully embraced the stages of space, clarity, direction, and action that led to the ride). Because of my foundation, and because I had dedicated intentional time to navigate my journey with therapists and coaches, I was not confused by my tears. I recognized the emotions I felt at my kitchen table were not of regret, but of love and understanding. I sobbed to grieve who I was, where I'd come from, and someone I still cared for. I cried to release what could have been—and that is okay.

Consider the ride not as a sign that something is off or that you should go back to what was. Consider the ride as a testament to how strong you are, to how much worth lies in your most expansive, authentic choices. Consider the ride as your invitation to experience more of life. Lastly, consider the ride not as an if but a when on your Alignment Journey.

Ride Practice One: Normalize the Ride

After taking action on your Alignment Journey, remind yourself of the ride. Rather than question whether your emotions and experiences are wrong, simply let them be. This part of the Alignment Journey is not for figuring out or understanding; this stage is simply to ride.

Allow grief to be a statement of respect; you enjoyed where you came from and you still care for your previous chapter. That does not mean you cannot turn the page.

Gift yourself compassion as you work through challenging times. Then, bask in moments that feel like a Yosemite lookout; fully taste experiences of hope and potential. Transfer these moments across areas of your life to foster confidence in your someday reality. Surrender when you arrive at ease.

As great and deep as your joys and sorrows may be, trust you are already steadfast in your truth. Trust your ride and trust it will be worth it.

YOU MAY WALK DOWNHILL BEFORE YOU SUMMIT

I introduced one of my clients in chapter four who had a gut feeling before we started working together that she wanted to quit her job. Her work was so emotionally draining, it took a toll on her most valued relationships. When she and I spoke for the first time, she was already burned out and overwhelmed.

Although her direction was clear, she was afraid. She was afraid of what this would mean for her finances. She was afraid of giving up on a career she once thought would be the one. She was afraid of starting over again after spending years getting to where she stood today.

We provided time during our first sessions together to enhance the first steps of her Alignment Journey: space, clarity, and direction. We explored these stages, not because she didn't know her career direction, but because her fears were powerful. She wanted reassurance that the action she was about to take was, indeed, her greatest alignment.

After a few rounds on the reassurance Ferris wheel, she was ready to set her fears aside and act. It was an exciting and momentous session—the session when she decided to quit.

We rehearsed what she would say to her beloved boss and returned to her why for clarity and extra motivation. "I want to be present for my partner and family again" was one of the most powerful drivers to take her leap.

A few days later, I received a message from her celebrating her official resignation. Tears were shed, nerves were embraced, and as it usually goes, she said the action step felt far less scary than the anticipation. We celebrated, and then I prepared to hold space as she entered the ride.

When her post-resignation ride began, she was caught off guard. As it is human for us to do, we tend to assume the grass is greener; we tend to imagine that when x happens, everything will change.

In some ways, this is true. My client relieved herself of the daily stress and burnout associated with her previous job.

She made it through the difficult resignation conversation and faced her fear of uncertainty head-on.

What led her to a place of burnout to begin with, however, would not disappear with the job. As you are invited to do on your own journey, she had to look within, heal, and create a new path forward—which welcomed its own challenges, shifts, and fields of possibility.

After her resignation, my client spent valuable time with family and her boyfriend; she followed through on her desire to restore close relationships. She took trips and visited with friends, redesigned her home office space, and watched Netflix.

Although we recognized how important these steps were to aid her burnout recovery and realign her foundation, fears appeared. She questioned her decision, doubted her future, and felt guilty resting even when there wasn't work to be done.

We created space amid the ride to reimagine who she was and what she truly desired. We removed the shoulds and the baggage from beliefs that no longer served her. We spent multiple sessions outlining her interests and potential career directions. One day, she sent me a job description she was elated to explore. It felt aligned with everything we'd illuminated about her preferences, ideal work environment, and skillset. She applied for the position with excitement and optimism.

At this point, the ride picked up momentum and added extra switchbacks for pizzaz. She didn't get the position.

This was heart-wrenching for both of us. Although I ultimately trusted this part of her journey as her coach, this reroute was particularly challenging. Her fears leaped at the chance to prove she had made the wrong choice.

But she had built a strong foundation of clarity, space, and direction. Her highest self knew she had not taken misaligned action, and this deeper knowing motivated her to stay on the path.

As she continued to create space, she was surprised to clarify graduate school as her next career step. With new insight came new action; she applied for and accepted a job at a wellness clinic and began her college applications.

This point marked our one year anniversary of working together—and while she still wasn't certain where she'd end up, she felt trust as she had now traversed the Alignment Journey multiple times and her next steps had come into focus.

Fortunately and unfortunately, the ride is like a stepping-stone path—except you can only see a few steps in front of you. Your answer-driven brain wants nothing more than to see the entire path clearly illuminated to the finish line.

We may lean on the adage I've referred to before for comfort: "It's about the journey, not the destination." Although beautiful, this statement excludes what said journey entails: a whirlwind of highs and lows, uncertainty and change.

As I wish for my clients, I hope you remember to fill your ride with enough celebration that the twists and turns feel worth it. Continuously refer back to your unshakable alignment foundation. And when gratitude and hope feel out of reach, please borrow my trust and confidence; in the end, your ride will be worth it.

MULTIPLE PATHS TO THE SUMMIT

Twists and turns along your ride not only manifest as emotional turbulence but as shifts in focus, as well. Although natural, most of my clients resist shifts in focus at this point on their journey. This resistance is often due to fear or worry that they are getting distracted; they do not see the big-picture connection between one area of life and the other, thus labeling their shift in focus as a diversion rather than a helpful detour.

One of my clients learned this lesson after strongly resisting her call to shift our focus from career goals to relationship alignment. (When this happened with me and my coach years ago, I resisted it, too.) For weeks, blips of her relationship story would surface during our coaching sessions—only for her to brush it off or insist we remain centered with how to incorporate her passion for coffee shops, cuisine, and yoga into one magical business venture.

Eventually, however, she surrendered; she begrudgingly trusted the topic that persistently called for her attention, and we dove in. At once, we felt the weight of resistance and mistrust lift. What followed was one of our most productive and insightful coaching sessions yet.

The beauty of these moments are glorious as you feel better both in allowing what is on your mind to be an adequate focus *and* in experiencing the results you craved in the first place. As my client finally opened herself and our coaching relationship to include her romantic life, she surrendered to the realization that her business alignment would clarify in its own time.

Relate this to the internal battle you experience when someone says, "Don't think about a yellow hippo." Your mind may attempt not to think about the topic at hand—but sometimes instinct is more powerful than willpower, and you think about it anyway.

When focus-shifting opportunities arise during your Alignment Journey, you have some autonomy to choose whether you will surrender to what seems to be a detour but could actually be the shortcut—or suppress what persistently calls for your attention.

Similarly, recenter with our previous discussions on discomfort. Sometimes, the Alignment Journey is not thrilling. It includes less comfortable experiences like grief, frustration, heartache, and fear. It includes tangents and uncertainty, paths you predicted and paths you never saw coming. But if you attempt to turn down the difficult, you will inevitably turn down the delicious as well.

A different client expressed this beautifully as she shared her six-month dream with me recently. She felt excited and inspired—feelings she was glad to have as we envisioned what was to come. Simultaneously, however, she courageously voiced her anticipation of hard work, fear, and worry.

"Of course!" I coached. Together, we shifted from a place of shame about her less comfortable emotions to a place of gratitude. All aspects of the Alignment Journey are a gift.

Cynthia Occelli offers a vibrant metaphor to illustrate the meaning of acceptance along your journey: "For a seed to achieve its greatest expression, it must come completely undone. The shell cracks, its insides come out, and everything changes. To someone who doesn't understand growth, it would look like complete destruction."

Your unexpected path, surprising shift in focus, or emotional ride may be exactly what you need at this point in the ride.

Better Than Your Predetermined Route

"I love this city…" I started to explain to my coach during our first session in over a month. "I'm proud of myself for leaving that misaligned project, and I'm grateful I had the resources to do it. Plus, I cannot believe I immediately landed an ideal job right away!"

I looked across my Saint Paul office to read "I love you" written on a notecard that rested against a framed photo of my family dog, Obi Wan. "And Tyler…" I continued on, "I am totally in love with Tyler. I leave for Thailand in three days to see him—and when I return, I'm excited to see what's next for my business…"

After listing everything that had transpired over the past two months, my coach replied with a chuckle and one word: "Wow." Then, silence.

I didn't have much else to say—but he could guess what came next. He had been my life coach for a year and knew more about the intimate details of my world than many others. My update made it seem like our work had culminated into one beautiful and perfect reality.

Certainly, from one perspective, this was true. Rewind to our previous coaching session when I sat in this same chair, looked around my office, and confidently (to my amazement) proclaimed, "I made it." (This part of the story will be expanded upon in the next stage of the Alignment Journey.) But that day, my inner response felt different from admiration or joy... instead, I felt sadness.

Although I was in awe of the life I had created, I never could have predicted it. I did not plan to leave my first evaluation project a few short months after excitedly committing. I did not anticipate accepting a full-time job three months after launching Yes&. I never would have guessed I'd enter a relationship with someone who would travel to Southeast Asia for an indefinite amount of time.

The *unplanned* nature of my fabulous life made me feel sad because part of me loves planning. This realization prompted me to question, "Is there a point to develop plans, goals, or aspirations if it never goes according to plan anyway?"

Through my own coaching session, I ultimately concluded the answer is yes. Because although my plans did not, and may never, unfold exactly as I intentionally conjure—my created vision serves as my guide toward a most remarkable life.

Ride Practice Two: Surrender to the Ride

Imagine yourself on switchbacks, slowly guiding you toward your mountain summit. Consider what occurs in nature as inspiration for your own ride—an experience you can fight against or embrace.

Practice compassion with yourself as you navigate your highs and lows. Trust each switchback will lead you closer to your desired summit, even when they lead you down-hill. To the best of your ability, accept your detour topics as they come. Release them just as easily, like clouds that drift overhead.

If it starts to feel overwhelming, feel that too, or seek additional support to create a safe space for you to explore. With compassion, frustration, and joy, it is all okay.

Keep Walking; You Are So Very Close

On my computer screen, I watched a contestant on *The X Factor* work fiercely with her painting on stage. The audience interpreted the painting as one of the judges—which prompted chuckles throughout the auditorium. With time, however, the audience's and judge's patience grew short. When the painting seemed to stop making progress, the judges announced their dissatisfaction with four loud red buzzers, forcing the artist to conclude her act.

My heart hurt as I watched the artist's face drop. Distraught, she drew a final line on her piece before setting her tools down—then gazed back to the audience to beg for their trust.

Although her time was up, the artist used another courageous minute to turn her canvas upside down. She threw powder over her creation to unveil one of the most impressive portraits I have ever seen.

The judges gave a standing ovation, and the audience erupted in applause. The show producers placed delighted music over the ending of this clip—as if to say, "everything worked out." I saw a different story.

My chest feels heavy and tears well in the back of my eyes no matter how many times I watch this act. There is a moving parallel to what happened with *The X Factor* artist and what happens in many of our Alignment Journeys.

I imagine your highest self as the artist in this clip, painting a masterpiece. The judges represent various aspects of you, from your creative child to your caring parent to your financial advisor. Your judges are well-intentioned, and they continuously seek assurance and proof that you fill your life with the best acts.

Sometimes, your judges eliminate an act "correctly." But what about moments like this? Moments when, had you just waited two more minutes, your artist could have flipped her canvas upside down and illuminated the most stunning piece of art you'd ever seen. What if you'd already buzzed her off stage?

Your Alignment Journey may not always feel crystal clear, especially during the ride. You will feel confused. You may become impatient. You will feel frustrated that it is not coming together as you had imagined or that it doesn't look gorgeous yet.

You must hold on long enough to allow your canvas to flip. With one brush of powder, your pieces will fall into place and you will witness absolute wonder for the life that stands in front of you.

Just as you created space to connect with your core… just as you dared to follow your clear heart by setting a direction and taking aligned action… you must also stand confidently in the fire of uncertainty, in the fire of your entire ride.

Do not hit your own buzzer. Do not lose hope due to ambiguity. Imagine your divine self working on your portrait, gazing back at you for two more minutes of trust. Embrace infinite possibility even if you do not see it—yet.

Trust. Trust. Trust… Very soon, you will cheer in total amazement upon your magnificent life's reveal.

Ride Practice Three: Trust

Trust. That is all.

Find something to hold onto. Keep your eyes open for your own Yosemite moment of reassurance. Create something in your moments of certainty and excitement to return to in moments of doubt and fear.

Take a deep breath and choose to trust. Your ride is worth it.

Gain access to over three additional practices to navigate the ride by downloading your Alignment Journey workbook at yesandbymarin.com/workbook.

CHAPTER 8

Enjoy the View: Celebrate Your Alignment

When do you celebrate? Perhaps after an important milestone: graduation, marriage, a work promotion… Perhaps after a fun experience: roller coaster cheer, theater applause, post-haunted house relief…

In our river metaphor, celebration may come most naturally once you arrive at the top of your mountain. I picture myself atop my first 13,000-foot climb with a huge smile across my face because I achieved something great.

Celebration is common in relation to achievement (every celebration above happens after something else occurs). In the sixth stage of the Alignment Journey, I emphasize the importance of celebration not only when you reach obvious milestones but every time you take one courageous step toward greater alignment.

Celebration is encouraged in the Alignment Journey with little victories, like when you remember to pause and breathe or when you say no to an opportunity everyone else would have labeled as the greatest celebration of all. Why? Because celebration feels fantastic, and because celebration fosters perseverance.

You know well by this point in your journey that alignment may not be an easy process, so it is important to discover what motivates you to remain on your journey. Furthermore, and simply, you deserve to feel good—especially when you choose what is best for you, and especially when others aren't ready to celebrate with you (yet).

Don't Pass by the Lookout

I stood on a rocky ledge overlooking the Mississippi River halfway through my run. I watched with intrigue as water flowed south, taking with it large branches and fallen leaves. My eyes shifted to the cliff adjacent to mine, and I wondered what it was like to be a university student in 2018.

The last time I stood in front of the Mississippi River, I was a university student myself. While it had only been a few years, my life felt dramatically different in comparison: I had graduated with my bachelor's degree in psychology, moved to California, and earned a master's degree in positive psychology; I'd spent hours driving up and down the California coastline to nurture my romantic relationship, only for it to end; I had fully, finally, recovered from my eating disorder; I made new, lifelong friends and gained a broader world perspective.

So much had changed in my life that it felt odd for the Mississippi overlook to look much the same. I considered it:

I was technically looking at different water, new university students, and fresh autumn leaves lining the horizon. My head spun as I began to consider our world as simultaneously consistent and ever changing.

Likewise, I was simultaneously consistent and ever changing. As reflected, my life changed over the course of three years—yet both three years ago and that day, I stood in the same spot mid-run, I felt ambition to pursue grand dreams, I felt challenged by my relationships, and I sometimes failed and sometimes succeeded to balance leisure with passionate work.

The cliffside moment was small, in the scheme of things. In total, it lasted no more than five minutes. I did not anticipate celebration to make an appearance that day, two miles into a leisurely run. I did not know what there was to celebrate.

Nonetheless, I followed my instinct to enjoy the lookout. I outstretched my arms parallel to the water's edge until my fingers began to tingle. I took a huge breath through my nose and lifted my sweat-stained face to the sky.

I took this stance partly because it felt right and partly because I've seen it done in the movies—and why not add a little extra drama? A smile rolled across my face and I celebrated feeling alive.

* * *

In March 2020, I began working with a new client at the same time as the Coronavirus pandemic shut down the United States. My client had two businesses at the time: one brick-and-mortar chiropractic office and one online wellness course. He hired me not only to navigate being a small business owner during uncertain times but to navigate change in the wake of divorce.

During our first session, he provided a short update about how he decided to finally close his chiropractic office and work full time on his true dream: an online wellness platform. He continued to speak, jumping immediately to what he thought we should cover during our first hour. More specifically, he started listing what he thought was wrong and needed to be worked through.

I stopped him in his tracks. "Hold on, you closed your chiropractic office!?" To be honest, I thought this action might not happen until one of our last months together. "You did the thing you've been too afraid to do for years?! And you made the decision to go all in on your dream of running an online wellness platform?!"

He chuckled as he realized what he'd glazed over. "Yeah, I suppose I did."

I illuminated just how big of a step he had taken. Closing the office he'd built for years was a bold and scary move, even though we both sensed it to be right for his next season. I invited us to take one minute, at least, to celebrate his huge victory. I cheered for him and felt pride on his behalf; I shared how powerful his step was to pave the way for what was to come and what this meant for the rest of our time together.

Between us deciding to work together and our very first session, this client had gone through one iteration of the Alignment Journey. He'd created space from his river, experienced clarity on shore, set his mountain direction, taken action on his path, and embraced the switchback ride. As is common for so many of us, he then wanted to jump right into his next Alignment Journey before embracing the last step: celebrate!

Some of my most deeply felt celebrations occur in moments where celebration was unwarranted or unexpected, like my cliffside, mid-run reflection or three minutes into my client's first coaching call. Of course, I am not condemning the celebration of weddings or graduations or home ownership. I've realized, however, we often do not give ourselves permission to celebrate the moments that lead up to and follow these milestones. It is vital to give yourself permission to celebrate everything.

Celebrate Practice One:
Always a Reason to Celebrate

Sometimes, it's not until you look back in hindsight that you realize how far you've come. One practice you can do right now, no matter where you are in your Alignment Journey, is to celebrate where you are at this moment.

Think of what you've accomplished already that brought you to where you sit today. Reflect upon the challenges you've already overcome, the events that have already transpired, and the growth you have already experienced.

As you become more comfortable in celebration, I challenge you to celebrate the mundane moments, as well, the moments when there isn't an obvious reason to celebrate.

One way I've incorporated this into my daily practice is through a morning gratitude journal. Writing five or more reasons I'm grateful each morning has opened my eyes to how much there is to be grateful for—and thus how much there is to celebrate. I celebrate that I have running water, that my dog is being patient instead of begging for the dog park, that the sun is out, or that the rain is nourishing our plants... I celebrate that I'm still working my dream job as a business owner and coach and that my clients continue to thrive. I celebrate waking up next to a man I love in a city that feels like home.

Celebrate the deliciousness of your iced mocha or the laugh lines on your face. Celebrate the birds that sing on a gorgeous summer day. Celebrate the shooting star you cheered for during a family bonfire. Celebrate yourself for taking rest. Celebrate being okay where you are, just as you are, for who you are—today.

FIND YOUR MILE MARKERS

It can feel challenging, or may be near impossible, to understand amid your journey how each event along the way fits together to create your desired outcome. In hindsight, however, you can say, "Ahhh, so that's why I didn't get the job of my dreams," or "This unexpected money was the catalyst to start my nonprofit."

What happens if you don't look back in hindsight?

Near the conclusion of our first coaching contract together, one of my clients called me with extra zest in her voice; she couldn't wait to tell me about an experience she'd had the previous weekend.

"Marin, I was driving in my car... it was raining, and I just got off the phone with my mom. We'd been arguing, again, and I was stressed about having enough time to work…"

So far, her story held a somber tone, but I could tell there was something coming by the energy behind her words.

"Historically, I would have rushed to work. I would have pushed through. I would have suppressed the conversation with my mom, or totally spun out about it. But guess what?"

She's celebrating, I recognized.

"I had a discussion with my mom about what was bothering me, and I kept the healthy boundaries we've been exploring in our recent coaching sessions while I listened to her perspective. And then…"

I already had a wide smile on my face. To anyone else, a conversation with mom may not feel big; as her coach, I knew it was life-changing.

"I journaled, Mar! I journaled in my car before work. I took a breath before work. And guess what!? I had plenty of time to finish what I needed."

She went on to explain this moment in her car on a rainy day felt like a culminating moment for our coaching work together. She felt like she'd been practicing for months to heighten her self-awareness, open herself to deep soul work, and practice vulnerability about what really mattered to her. In the car on that day, all her hard work paid off; she embraced the opportunity to implement the version of her new, intentional self. And she celebrated.

These are the moments I live for as a coach: moments of aha and gratitude, moments where it clicks, moments when life is not only anticipated to be greater but is experienced as greater than my clients ever imagined.

Just as in my own cliffside story, these moments are often mundane. My client wasn't nearly as excited to tell me about her six-figure business year (although she'd accomplished that, as well)—she was excited to tell me she journaled in her car after a hard conversation with her mom.

My client celebrated a new life, not a new achievement. She celebrated that a situation arose just like it had one hundred times before, and instead of reverting to old storylines, limiting beliefs, and unhelpful mindsets, she trusted and implemented something new—and this something new felt right. It felt aligned.

Six-figure business years are also worthy of celebration—and shifting decade-old behaviors to create a new outcome that feels amazing? That is worthy of celebration, too.

Another beautiful example comes from a client who named self-love as her coaching priority. During our first session together, I held space as she opened her heart to showcase the worries, fears, and shame she'd historically kept hidden. We spent months putting one false belief after another to rest. We practiced small acts of self-love like feeling worthy of her first-class seat on an airplane and cooking delicious food for herself at home. By the end of our time together, my client's testimonial included the statement, "I feel content and powerful in my own life."

I treasure my final session with clients because it builds in an opportunity to celebrate. I remind my clients to take a pause and consider how far they've come. I am there, both as a coach and a time-marker, to give them a reason to reflect and a reason to rejoice.

Furthermore, I purely enjoy this last session with clients because I give them permission to feel pride and admiration—feelings many of us reserve for others rather than mirror ourselves.

Celebrate Practice Two:
Build Milestones Into Your Journey

You may feel pressured to run from one accomplishment to the next—or do so instinctually—scurrying to accomplish your next task or set your eyes on a new milestone before fully celebrating what you just achieved. While I'm all for forward momentum, remind yourself to create moments of gratitude along the way.

As I shared in the story with my clients, it often takes something external for us to notice our developments and accomplishments. Use this awareness to intentionally build celebration into your journey. Create your own milestones, even if they seem arbitrary; you needn't wait for a "legitimate" reason to pause, reflect, and celebrate.

Set a reminder in your phone to go off every month, or every six months, or once a day to reflect on how far you've come. Reserve space in your calendar at the end of each week to celebrate the goals you accomplished, the lessons you learned, and the unexpected gifts that fell into your lap. Create a reward board and gift yourself bonuses for your hard work and milestones reached.

If you opt for the reward board, as with all built-in celebrations, remind yourself that you are worthy of celebration regardless. Therefore, include a gift or two for you to accept at random along your journey—just because you are undoubtedly stupendous already.

Cheer Your Triumph Into the Valley

This stage of the Alignment Journey would not be complete without a short conversation about narcissism. Being narcissistic is one of the most common hesitations voiced by my clients for why they do not want to celebrate their personal journey.

In my dorm room sophomore year, I pinned a quote by Marianne Williamson above my bed: "As we let our own light shine, we unconsciously give other people permission to do the same." At the time, I hung the quote on my wall as a reminder that someone else believes this to be true—and maybe, one day, I would, too.

Today, as I draft this chapter of the Alignment Journey, I am seated in front of a fireplace in a northern Wisconsin cottage. It is early fall. Raindrops dance down the windows beside me. Lake Michigan roars with the wind outside. I am writing my first book—a dream come true and an event my high school social studies teacher predicted years ago. Tomorrow, I have a speaking event in collaboration with someone I admire, and I just received a kind and excited note from an interested client.

Today, as I write this chapter on celebration, I have a lot to celebrate. I am living my dream life, and I am incredibly inspired by myself for creating it. I take a moment to bask in this feeling of joy, admiration, and pride for myself—and I invite you to do the same for your own life.

Aware that hundreds or thousands of individuals may read these words, I feel myself shy away from celebrating myself too much. A little voice may enter your mind, as well, amid celebration: "Am I being narcissistic?"

If this question arises, ask it for real. Are you being narcissistic? If a friend celebrated what you wish to celebrate for yourself in this moment, would you call them narcissistic?

Although narcissism is not something to take lightly, it is more often than not a false worry for individuals pursuing greater self-awareness and authentic alignment. (Would a narcissistic individual ask themselves if they were being narcissistic?)

By living in alignment with this false fear, you are not only hindering your ability to fully and joyously experience the authentic life you've created throughout your journey—you are inhibiting others from pursuing and celebrating their own. "As we let our own light shine, we unconsciously give other people permission to do the same."

Celebrate Practice Three:
Address the Narcissistic Gremlin

When was the last time you beamed with pride for someone else? Call to mind a moment of celebration for one of your friends, colleagues, or family members.

Then, consider the fear of narcissism from a different perspective: If or when your friend celebrated in your memory, did you feel neglected? Did others around them feel less than because of their celebration? What would have happened if this individual did not permit celebration in this scenario—would the world be a better place?

Once you've critically considered narcissism through the lens of a friend, use your exploration to inform how it feels best to celebrate yourself while maintaining alignment with your other values (such as family, friendship, and respect).

As a little extra encouragement, please let me remind you: You are unlike any other human on this earth. Your unique purpose is essential to the vibrancy of our world just as much as my own thriving or that of anyone else. No matter what you have or have not done, no matter how many sales you've made or milestones you've met, you are worthy of celebration right now.

STAND YOUR CHOSEN GROUND

One season that naturally prompts celebration is the holidays. Families come together, friends catch up after long stints away, gifts are exchanged, and magical snow covers trails along the lakes in the Midwest.

In addition to feel-good holiday celebrations, however, there is an infusion of sought-after and forced celebration. Relatives ask how business is going in anticipation of good news. Parents ask college-age kids about classes with hope for straight A's and their next-step plan. Friends ask the newlyweds when we can expect a baby.

Many of us feel pressure to not only have something to celebrate in our holiday conversations but to have something to celebrate that others deem worthy of celebration. Opinions splatter about who has lost weight, who received a huge promotion, and "When are you getting married?"

"Are you working?" "When will I have grandkids?" "Have you graduated yet?"

These questions are intended well; it is normal to ask for an update, especially from people you do not often see. It is normal to look ahead in anticipation of the new year. And you know what is also normal? To choose a different path, to make mistakes, and to exist in seasons of contentment between seasons of growth and change.

If you feel pressured to celebrate, be it at holidays, work social hours, or on the phone with your parents, return to your compass and remind yourself what *you* desire to celebrate. Allow it to be good enough.

Celebrate who you are at this moment. Honor what *you* choose to focus on. Embrace your authentic decisions and shine self-trust upon the world with confidence.

Embrace your update to the family that you are no longer in a relationship, or no longer working with someone else's dream company, or no longer interested to live nearby. Proclaim proudly your promotion, big successes, and highlights. Share all of this, regardless of how your aunt responds to your career change, regardless of the fears unintentionally (or intentionally) shared with you in response, and regardless of what anyone else deems worthy.

Of course, there is a time and place; read the room, and carefully consider whether there are some aspects of life you choose not to celebrate with family and friends. When needed, draw boundaries to safe-harbor your light so it can shine even brighter where it feels best—rather than deplete it in environments that make it hard to glow.

My point is this: you have permission to show up just as you are. Smile with freedom and glow, if that is what lives in your core. See the beauty, the possibility, and the love that is already. Shine light upon the incredible that surrounds you, no matter if it looks different than you thought it would and no matter if you long for something else in the future—and remain unapologetic about following your truth.

MOTIVATION TO PERSEVERE THROUGH ANOTHER CLIMB

Celebration feels good—but it seems this reason alone does not satisfy the question of *why* to celebrate.

In chapter six, I shared my story about the time I reflected with my coach about my unplanned, gorgeous reality. I mentioned that a month prior I had experienced an "I made it" moment. This is it:

I sat in my desk chair with earbuds in and my phone on my lap. My coach was on the other line. My desk in front of me was covered in notes for the weekly video I had filmed an hour earlier. The camera I used still rested on my mom's old travel tripod in front of my single office window.

As I looked around, my office felt disheveled, especially for my typically well-organized self. But as I took in the mess, I smiled as I considered why: because I was doing it. The stuff scattered around my office indicated I was creating something that was once just a dream: running a full-time coaching business.

I had originally prepared to talk to my coach about a feel-good business structure to bring in consistent income.

Once I paused, however, I realized my worry in and of itself illuminated the celebration I had forgotten to experience: I am a full-time business owner.

At first, a messy desk might not seem worthy of celebration—but it was. I may not have hit my first six-figure year, or written my first best-selling book, or filled my client roster. But I *had* made my dream a reality. I said yes to what I cared about—and said no to what I did not. I was doing the thing I once longed to do.

On the phone with my coach that day, I celebrated with three delightfully surprising words: "I made it." Not only did this statement feel freaking good, it provided inspiration and motivation to persevere through the challenging days, months, and weeks ahead.

If you never celebrate your accomplishments or reflect to see how far you've already come, you may believe you haven't made any progress at all. If you've made it this far in the Alignment Journey, that is most certainly false.

Celebrate Practice Four: Give Yourself a Gift

Prevent burnout and gift yourself a feel-good moment by taking time to experience the glorious reality of your present moment. Intentionally thank yourself for whatever it took to get you to this point. Take a step back from what anyone else deems as "making it" or worthy of celebration to ask yourself: what is there to celebrate now?

Will you celebrate taking a courageous leap? Will you celebrate taking action? Will you celebrate reaching a milestone *you* deem important? Will you celebrate choosing to live in alignment, regardless of your external circumstances?

Find a reason to celebrate each step along the way rather than reserving celebration for special occasions. Savor your experiences not only at the end of each Alignment Journey but in the midst of your journey. Celebrate dreams you've manifested already, just as you celebrate dreams you look forward to in the future.

I would love to celebrate with you! Celebrate a current win by gifting yourself the support of coaching for future wins! Learn how at yesandbymarin.com/experience.

Gain access to over ten additional practices to celebrate your alignment by downloading your Alignment Journey workbook at yesandbymarin.com/workbook.

CHAPTER 9

Discover More: Begin Again

What about when life doesn't go according to plan?

You get married and end your partnership one (or forty) years later. You earn a degree and, upon completion, realize your passion lies elsewhere—or the universe guides you toward a seemingly unrelated career. You courageously move cross-country and do not love the town you excitedly anticipated for years. You let down your guard in a friendship, and your vulnerability is not reciprocated. You hit a deer on the highway and find yourself without a car and with a great financial bill...

With our river metaphor, the stage of the Alignment Journey we are about to enter is one of beginning again: summiting your mountain, only to realize there is another one to climb. Or reaching your sought-after lookout only to learn you now desire something new.

Confusion, frustration, anger, sadness, relentless ambition, release...

Many emotions follow the unplanned. The unknown is scary, and feeling out of control is uncomfortable. What if there was a hack to navigate the inevitable unexpected turns of your Alignment Journey?

"This wasn't the plan" implies there was a plan to begin with—likely, there was a sense of control; you had a vision, an intention, a desire, and thus your unexpected event or outcome felt like something was taken from you. "It's not fair."

Step one to navigate the unexpected is to honor your emotions and natural reactions. These are crucial messengers to guide your understanding of what you value, desire, and believe. If you feel hurt, there is also care. If you feel confused, a long-held belief may be in question. If you are fighting to sustain your initial plan, the linked outcome is something you still long for.

"It's not fair." "This wasn't the plan." "I don't have the resources to deal with this." Go there. Give yourself permission to feel it all—and remain curious. Remember, emotions rarely overwhelm you for more than a few minutes when you allow yourself to feel them completely, so if you feel safe and supported, you can go to the depth of this emotion and simply let it be.

Step two to navigate the unexpected turns of your Alignment Journey is to release your immediate reaction. It will come, and when it does, take a breath to remind yourself change is all there is.

Feel compassionate toward your frustration and then... Let it go. Adapt. Shift. Move. Release your fight against reality, allow what is, and begin again.

WHEN YOU THOUGHT THE LOOKOUT WAS THE PEAK

One of my clients spent months redefining her role in her music school business; she desired the role of a CEO, which eventually expanded further to "I desire to be the face of this company" rather than a worker within it.

Her dreams were admirable and exciting. Furthermore, they were within her reach. She had already built a team of support around her to take care of administrative tasks and teaching lessons.

As is common with most of my clients (which likely means this is your case, as well), the biggest hurdle my client had to overcome was the story she'd created inside her mind.

Through coaching, we ventured through her Alignment Journey by creating space for the elaborate story about having to work harder and keep her hands dirty to be a good leader. We clarified her desired role and vision, set her new direction, and started taking action.

The ride included celebrations and hardships, as it always does. Within a few months, she had successfully made the transition from teacher to leader and was enjoying more time with her son at home. She sent me a picture of herself in Paris, with the purse she promised herself in honor of her wildly successful year.

Then, a pandemic rocked small businesses around the world. Her in-person music school closed. As countless others were forced to do during the year of 2020, she led her team to shift from in-person classes to virtual instruction as quickly as possible.

Although she demonstrated great leadership throughout this shift, the sudden change also prompted many of her old storylines to reenter her mind. I heard a flood of overwhelm flow over her as she reacted to the state of our world: "Now I have to teach all the online classes! I finally had it figured out, and now I have to start over!"

My client is not the only one to voice this type of frustration along her Alignment Journey. Whether it's conscious or not, many of us adopt the belief that, one day, we'll figure it all out. We believe one day, we'll arrive; one day, we will no longer be in a cycle of personal and professional development. One day, we will be fully developed—with our dream life in front of us, challenges overcome, and a sense of success and resolution.

I, too, believe this is true. There will come a day when it all falls into place and you feel concluded... but that day isn't when you finally get the promotion, become the CEO you always dreamed to be, or marry on a scenic mountain altar. Resolution starts and ends within your own mind and is surprisingly independent of the external events in your life.

Further, it is our human instinct to evolve and move. Thus, you will always look toward another step, long for the next milestone, discover a new area to grow, and accept a new challenge to overcome. The day you stop doing this is the day you stop living.

My client figured it out for a blip of time, and you bet we celebrated—and it did not surprise me when her conceivably overcome stories resurfaced.

The visual I share with my clients is one of an upward spiral. Although you may revisit old storylines, challenges, or beliefs, you do so at a different layer than you have in the past; you may revisit similar lessons, but you do so at a new level of understanding. Your ability to uplevel arises not only when you access new challenges and experiences but when you access old challenges and experiences with new eyes and a developed arsenal of tools you hadn't created before.

My client had already navigated her work-harder, do-it-all story once. Now it was not a matter of rewriting her story but remembering what she'd already written.

Do not get discouraged when you, too, experience moments of having it all followed by moments of revisited challenge. This is growth, and you are more capable than ever to journey through it.

Even the Best Trained Climbers Falter

Previously in this book, I shared how I spent months in preparation to adopt a dog. I went on walks as if I already owned a pup. I read a dog training book, adopted a lens of positive reinforcement and patience, and repeated the mantra, "There is always enough time."

Planner Marin had it all under control... until my dog didn't abide by the plans.

I adopted a dog in September of 2019, and shortly thereafter, I was faced with an unexpected reality. Aatto didn't want to go on walks at 3 p.m. and train at 5, he wanted to run at the dog park first thing in the morning and train in short five-minute bursts. In fact, walks weren't much help at all; Aatto needed much more stimulation to exert his pent up herding energy.

I was patient with this shift at first because "it only takes six weeks to train a dog if I follow this book..." But six weeks came and went, and I realized I needed to adopt a new lifestyle for the long haul.

I thought I'd engrained the belief "there is always enough time"—but as I experienced the reality of dog ownership, I realized I had written fine print underneath the belief: "There is always enough time, as long as I can plan my time." "There is always enough time, as long as I can anticipate what time I have." "There is always enough time, and there is a right order to organize activities within it."

I self-coached my way through the Alignment Journey. I created space to feel my frustration, worry, joy, and love I felt with Aatto. I clarified why my frustration existed in the first place (because my daily plan never went accordingly... because it was totally unrealistic). I set a new direction based on new data points (e.g., Aatto needs exercise first thing in the morning). I took action to implement our new routine, and I navigated the accompanying ride that followed.

After going through my mini Alignment Journey, I felt pretty good. I had it figured out.

The surprise that followed wasn't one of greater challenge or spiral learning but total joy and trust. Not only had I adjusted to create a daily schedule and dog-mom routine that worked, I learned my new schedule felt better than any schedule I'd adopted in the past. I reached my mountain peak expecting a decent view, only to experience the most gorgeous overlook I could imagine.

Being a dog mom challenged me to let go of many perfectionistic tendencies. It invited me to consider different lifestyle choices that in turn evoked greater life balance. Aatto and his cute face invited me to accept what is—rather than fight against reality and push my motives and preconceived ideals onto a mismatched truth. I experienced the magic of working with what I found at my summit.

At the introduction of the Alignment Journey, I emphasized the process as nonlinear and continuous. Understanding this concept and experiencing it are two different things. To feel like you finally made it, only to realize there is more room for growth, discovery, and life, can be frustrating—unless you consider these moments as simply part of the journey. Hold space for change and newness to enter your journey, as it inevitably will, and stay present to what is.

Begin Again Practice One: Normalize Surprise

If you assume nothing goes according to plan, rather than assume your plans will always go accordingly... how would it change your life? Could you invoke a sense of freedom instead of frustration?

Reflect upon a plan that has since been enacted in your life—a vacation, your career path, your journey to parent-hood, or your goal to put away the dishes by the end of the night. What was your original plan, and what surprise did your original plan *not* anticipate?

What did you feel when the surprise entered your plan—and how did your reaction help you or set you farther back? How did the surprise *benefit* your journey?

Alternatively, have you ever created a plan that went off without a hitch—exactly as anticipated? How was that experience? Was it better than instances when plans in-cluded surprise?

WHEN THE MOUNTAINSIDE IS SLICK

Now that you have normalized surprise endings in your Alignment Journey, let's build a toolkit for what to do when you arrive: begin again.

I was introduced to the concept of begin again by my mentor Coby Kozlowski in 2014. She invited us to play a game that requires frequent restarts—and each time we restarted, we had the opportunity to say, "Begin again!"

At times, begin again was voiced through gritted teeth. At others, it was cheered with exuberance and zest, as if we'd won the opportunity to play one more time.

As I played and reflected with Coby's begin-again game, I learned two valuable lessons. First, I can always begin again. Second, it is my choice to celebrate or dread the process when I do.

It's been years since Coby first introduced me to begin again, and since her introduction, I've seen others' interpretation of this masterful concept as well. Today, I guide myself, my clients, and you to welcome it into our journey as much as possible—such as in October of 2019, when I wrote in my evening journal: "Today was a Begin Again day."

My day had ended on the opposite side of the universe from where it began. I roasted chickpeas twice—because I forgot my first batch in a 400-degree oven for an hour (and a half...) longer than instructed. I ate ice cream for breakfast *and* had a fantastic workout at noon. I went from mindlessly scrolling YouTube to energetically crafting my next big dream.

Whether it is within a game, amid a project, or capturing an entire day, begin again is your reminder that *you* are the only one standing in your way—which also means you alone are capable of creating something extraordinary.

You do not need an excuse; you do not need a new day, a new year, a different season, or someone else's permission to shift. You alone hold the power to accept what is and move forward. Even if you have a horrendous morning, you do not need to burn the rest of your day to the ground or pop three tires just because one is flat.

One of my clients spent months preparing, marketing, and anticipating the launch of his first online course. This course was not only the first online product he'd created but a huge milestone in creating his dream business after closing his chiropractic office (I told the first piece of his story earlier).

During one of our sessions, he explained feeling like "it all rides on this launch." After exploring the belief, he realized the all-or-nothing statement wasn't truthful; it was based out of fear and scarcity. Nonetheless, he remained hopeful for the momentum this launch could create for his business and new life.

We concluded our session one week before the big day. I looked forward to connecting with him again seven days later to hear about the outcome.

"Well," he started our next call, "I still believe in this, and I can shift some things, and…"

I hadn't heard the outcome yet, but he was already justifying, reacting, and planning for something better.

"No one bought the course," he broke.

As a coach, I care deeply for my clients—especially those who commit to working with me one-on-one. When I begin a coaching relationship with a new client, I tell them to consider me as their person for the next six months. I don't take this lightly.

I am their person through all the highs and all the lows; I am their person through the confusion and vulnerability; I am their person when questions feel hard, and I am their person when exciting revelations come with ease.

When my client told me no one had purchased his course, I held space with him. I invited us to take a breath together. I invited his planner mind to lay it all out there, as was his natural inclination to do so. Then, I invited him to take a step back and welcome the emotional part of him to speak.

I felt his breath and shoulders drop on the other side of the phone. "I am tired."

Just as we gave voice to the planner part of himself, we explored which part of him was finally able to speak. The name that felt aligned with his tired feeling was the Caregiver. This part of him had been taking care of everyone *else*, and when we asked this part of him what he needed, he replied simply: "I need to take care of myself."

This type of insight is profound, though off-putting to what some of us have grown accustomed to. My client's instinct was to react to his zero-sale launch and start planning for the next, better step. Instead, I guided my client to take a breath and find true resolve in this cycle of the journey by beginning again. Once he leaned into this, we naturally revisited stage one of the Alignment Journey—which is not to act or plan. The beginning of the Alignment Journey is to notice we are in a river and create space.

Remember the metaphor, chapters ago, about taking one breath after the other without space in between? You needn't take action immediately after your previous Alignment Journey concludes. In fact, it is often detrimental to react in place of taking wise, aligned action.

Just as my client did, begin again by creating space. Pause. Breathe. Feel your emotions. Process where you came from—a new river, a new landscape, a new experience.

To the planners and go-getters out there itching to take action, trust that action is coming. Action has its rightful place in the Alignment Journey, as well. And right now, you have permission to take a step back and rest.

The More You Journey the Easier It Gets

Early in our coaching relationship, one of my clients was obviously uncomfortable with surprises. I distinctly recall one of our first sessions together: she called me, frantically, a few minutes late. Her newborn son had been crying. Work needed to get done. Nonetheless, she prioritized our coaching call because in her gut she knew it was important.

While clients typically enjoy taking coaching calls in a quiet room at home, this client opted to pace her neighborhood sidewalks to alleviate the discomfort of sitting still— and to distance herself from the reminders of chaos at home.

Although this frantic energy became a theme throughout many of our early sessions together, we grew compassionate toward it. Using the caricature lesson introduced to you in chapter three, she named her frantic, problem-solving, go-getter personality Punky Brewster.

Whenever a surprise entered my client's Alignment Journey, Punky Brewster jumped into the driver's seat in a panic and threw her personal and professional life out of balance and off course. We spent multiple sessions unraveling this pattern, rewiring surprises as part of the journey to expect—rather than a failure to avoid—and realigned with her higher self as the intentional driver of her life.

A few months into our work together, she no longer felt frantic and stressed if she was late to a session. Instead, if she ran late, she would text me her expected time of arrival. Once on the line, she entered our conversations with full trust that our time together was always valuable, and whatever happened leading up to our call was okay. In fact, staying present with her life, rather than running through it, became one of her most cherished practices to experience fulfillment and foster strength in herself as a mother and CEO.

One year into our coaching relationship, her growth from fearing surprise to embracing life shined. She received a phone call in the middle of a coaching session from her boyfriend. She kindly asked if she could take the call, to which I said, "Of course, what is best for you is best for me." While I waited in my office for her to return, she and her boyfriend entertained a ten-minute argument—yet I wouldn't have picked that up had she not told me about it.

Once she called me back, I held space as she naturally leaned into her feelings—sensing a part of her, Punky Brewster, wanting to derail our original coaching focus to vent about the argument that just took place. She recognized many of the stories she *could* choose to spiral out over felt historic and unnecessary. Most importantly, she did all of this without judgment, shame, or force.

With awareness, she ultimately chose to recenter with the clarity and direction she'd set for our session thirty minutes earlier.

I watched in amazement as the same client—who at one point allowed Punky Brewster to argue in favor of old storylines for half a session—noted her stories as interesting observations, and nothing more. With compassion, she named the characters and outdated reactions from the place of her higher self. She listened to the characters' perspectives enough to calm them down and hear their concerns and ultimately released them in favor of her true and most present desires.

Within a few minutes, we returned to her original focus for the session: a celebration of her recent, incredible business achievements. Along with it, however, we added in one of the greatest celebrations to date: her ability to begin again—in real time—with great compassion and awareness, and with surprising ease.

This story is a gorgeous representation of how begin again transforms over time. Although it may feel awkward and unnatural at first, trust the growth and awareness you will experience as your journey repeats. With time, you, too, will find your groove and natural desire to choose to begin again.

Look to the Sky for Inspiration

The previous client story emphasized my client's newfound ability to flow with change rather than fight against it. One of my favorite reminders to practice this type of flow is available to most all year long: the seasons.

I have always loved the seasons, and for a long time, I assumed this was simply because of the unique experience each season brings; I assumed I was drawn to the changing colors, varied temperatures, and obvious shift from sparkling Christmas lights to driveway car washes on a warm summer day. Although these experiences are, indeed, marvelous, I realized with time my attraction to seasons went far deeper than a visceral observation.

My love for the seasons expanded once I experienced the consistent, sunny days of California during graduate school. For me, this perfect-day weather also prompted an expectation for everything else to be perfect—including myself. Especially during the demands of graduate school, identical sunny days made me believe I had to show up as an identical perfect student every single day.

Conversely, during my undergraduate education in Minnesota, I experienced a necessary difference in my studies. When the breeze and sunshine provided a comfortable atmosphere of focus, I enjoyed working on the front steps of the library. When negative temperatures and blizzard snow appeared, I used my school's underground tunnels and cozied up with my work in a library study nook or stayed home.

In California, I reflected on my seasonal years with a type of nostalgia few of my local friends understood. "But this weather is perfect," they insisted—as did the rest of the state.

One December afternoon, I drove to a local coffee shop, ordered a hot peppermint mocha, and parked with my air conditioning on blast. It didn't seem like my birthday without snow on the ground and Christmas lights on dusted pine trees, so I did my best to replicate them. "How did sunshine and blue skies become the nation's definition of perfect?" I pondered.

Here's what I came up with: southern California weather was linked with ease, comfort, and predictability. None of these identifiers were bad or wrong, but I wasn't convinced they defined perfect weather.

In the Midwest, I experienced a comradery among individuals who embrace the cold winters and wild temperature fluctuations. Our co-experienced laughter as we brushed snow off our fall jackets in the cafe was a way of nodding to the unpredictability and uncontrollable nature of life. Rainy days prompted evenings on our couches with friends and a movie instead of our originally intended campfire, snowstorms canceled plans or elicited alternative, creative solutions… And through it all, we were forced to acknowledge that life isn't always golden—and that was okay. In fact, in my experience, most of us believed it to make life a little more beautiful.

Negative-fifty-degree weather accompanied with snow-covered highways may not be everyone's cup of tea. For me, however, the surprising fluctuations in seasons are closer to perfect because they represent life, and the Alignment Journey, exquisitely.

With every seasonal change or surprise forecast, we have the opportunity to embrace the current moment, recognize change as ordinary, and invite a new perspective. In other words, we have the opportunity to begin again.

Begin Again Practice Two:
Find Begin Again in Your Life

Whether you are in the midst of an unexpected business outcome, abrupt surprise, or natural change, invite yourself to adopt a mindset of begin again.

When you encounter such change, what inspires you to enter another round of the Alignment Journey? What about beginning again feels fantastic? How might you shift your relationship with beginning again to embrace a little more ease, trust, and joy along your journey?

Lastly, what experiences around you, such as a change of season, will remind you to begin again at the conclusion of a journey?

There Is More to Venture

It is human nature to crave completion; we crave a story arc that brings us back to where we began. Our brains automatically depict a picture from abstract clouds or fill the spaces in a paint by number—because absolution and conclusiveness feel safer than unnamed chaos.

So start with compassion for the part of you that desires 100% confidence and absolute assurance. Your desire is human.

Then, consider this: an invented answer provides the same calm for your mind as one of truth. Use this power to ease unnecessary suffering—because sometimes, the most beautiful gift you can give yourself is permission to make believe.

Otherwise, you could spend a lifetime questioning whether you should have been a doctor, wondering what went wrong in that friendship, considering whether it was a mistake to move away from this city…

Your mind can and will replay your stories again and again and again in anticipation for the grand finale—the part where you reach resolution. And if a concluding storyline doesn't show, your brain will hit rewind to find the certain answer you must have missed, to make sense of what feels chaotic or abstract.

If you are currently experiencing this torturous cycle in an area of your life, you may be stuck on an option you do not wish to let go of: a career you still desire, unfinished business between you and a significant person... Beginning again by choosing the option you at one time dismissed could provide your craved resolution to this particular Alignment Journey. If this feels true for you, by all means do it.

Quite possibly, however, your spinning mind may simply illuminate your desire for conclusion of any kind. If that feels more true for you, you have permission to make it up.

Resolution exists in your ability and willingness to decide. Either begin again by choosing, today, to shift careers in favor of the alternative you constantly circle back to or reaching out to the person you wish you had spoken to a decade ago... Or decide you will not.

Conclude your circular story in your mind. Gift yourself the freedom to create a reason it didn't work out. Take notice of how wonderful your current circumstance turned out to be—and believe in your resolve wholeheartedly.

Stop creating suffering where it needn't be. Choose to let go of the past. Leave your mental continuum of "if only..." Abandon what could have been to realize what can be.

You have more life to live, beyond the heartbreak or regret or hurt or confusion. Learn from it. Respect it. Permit it. And then release it. Decide, and move on.

There is always more to come—so begin again.

LEAVE NO ONE BEHIND

I hope you recognize my invitation for you to make up resolution is not an invitation for you to turn a blind eye to data and reality. Rather it is an invitation for you to stop believing the alternative, made-up story in your mind that imprisons you in a dead zone—or an outdated factory.

Recently, I was on the phone with my coach when we unearthed a gorgeous visual to depict my current life: a shiny, new factory. In my mind, it was sparkly, blue, and bright. Abundant workers impersonated different versions of myself, and all of them excitedly and passionately completed their unique tasks. In my factory, there was a music room, a therapy room, and a museum—which held all the stuff I didn't want to fully let go of… but knew didn't fully belong in my new factory, either.

Although it was invigorating to unveil this metaphorical factory, I also sensed it wasn't running at full capacity—and this bummed me out! If every part of my shiny new factory was working efficiently, the possibilities I could create in my life were limitless.

As I stayed curious about this metaphor with my coach, we eventually unveiled a *second* factory—an old factory across the street. Parts of me, and thus some factory workers, were still at the dusty, outdated factory working under old beliefs in a historic reality.

Through story, we invited my old factory workers to tour the new place—and to my surprise, they jumped at the opportunity with wide, excited eyes. Then, when we invited the old factory workers to grab their stuff and move across the street, my imaginary workers nearly danced on the tables.

The day after my coaching session, I thought about this new factory and nearly danced on the kitchen table myself;

it felt exciting, like a big shift was coming. I felt like I was finally all in on my new life, rather than tethered to an old version of me. I felt different, in the best way possible.

Do I believe there is a factory in my brain with a bunch of mini-Marin's running around, taking breaks in the therapy room, sipping cold brew coffee in the break room, and excitedly working on new tasks? No, not exactly. And... walking through this metaphorical story with my coach shifted something real inside of me.

By telling the story of an old factory, I noticed parts of me were still working under old conditions; parts of me were completing inefficient or completely ineffective tasks; parts of me were simply sitting still in nostalgia and believed there was nothing more to do.

When I invited these workers to join the bright, shiny blue workspace... I invited all parts of me to fully enter the version of my life that is most present, true, and expansive. Then, by closing down the old factory altogether and inviting the universe to bulldoze it and make it into a park for kids (yes, life coaching gets weird...), I chose to release my old stories, beliefs, and connections.

This is what I mean when I say make up your own resolution. Do what you have to do to step into the best version of yourself. By all means, please take responsibility for who you are and how you impact those around you. And stop clutching BS stories and perspectives that ultimately *only* live inside your head.

Begin Again Practice Three:
Make It Up so You Can Keep Moving

Celebrate your ability to begin again as an opportunity to live your best, most powerful, and expansive life. Your best life is possible today no matter where you came from, no matter what you have or have not already learned, and no matter how many times you've spiraled down the same storyline.

Celebrate that begin again is a thing in the first place. Embrace it in all its new factory-old factory weirdness. Celebrate being aware of a begin-again moment by cheering, "Yahoo! Begin again!"

Lastly, dare to adopt the belief that you can begin *now*—rather than tomorrow, or next paycheck, or after you lose the weight. Begin again. And again. And again. And again. Now and for the rest of your life.

A Switchback Is Not a Circle

As I worked toward making the decision to start my own business, I held the conscious (and at times subconscious) belief that I wasn't capable of earning enough money to support myself through Yes& alone: "I can't afford *not* to have a real job."

At first, I embodied this belief by applying for full-time evaluation work during my final year of graduate school. I proudly embraced all the right preparations: I networked with other evaluators, beautified my resume, completed informational interviews, and set forth an application plan that ensured ample opportunity to secure a job by graduation.

It soon became obvious that a full-time evaluation job was not an ideal next move for me—as showcased by my absolute lack of enthusiasm to write a cover letter or prepare for an interview, let alone dedicate forty hours a week to this work. I felt empowered to pursue a career I was more passionate about, instead.

I began again, courageously set my job applications aside, and declared I would open my own business as a coach full time.

Alignment Journey complete, right?

Of course not. Long-held beliefs, likely adopted with the intention of ensuring safety, will do everything they can to survive. Just as flu viruses do year after year, my belief simply adapted.

After graduating with my master's degree *without* an evaluation job lined up, I enacted a plan to launch my coaching business by September 1, 2018. I hired a branding coach to set my business structure during the summer and worked enthusiastically to organize every logistical detail of my dream—including financial goals based on my data-informed budget. I considered my average spending, cost of living, and envisioned lifestyle. Then, I asked: "How will I afford it all?"

Excel spreadsheet in hand, I laid out the *how* behind my income and spending: "If I charge this much for coaching, I will need this many clients a month…" The problem arose when I realized my ideal client load was far less than the required numbers. Almost without thought, I then added one more line on my financial plan: "I'll supplement some income with part-time evaluation work!"

I defended this addition because my evaluation work would "only be part time." I adopted beliefs to back up the sense in my decision: "It takes a while for new businesses to see profit… This will give me time to set a strong foundation for my business… Additional income will alleviate pressure from Yes&…

The week before my official launch of Yes&, I was offered an evaluation opportunity that met my requirements exactly, and I accepted the position. It also matched my persistent, limiting belief: "I cannot afford *not* to have a real job."

My "perfect" manifestation crumbled a few months later; although the position provided financial security, it did not foster my well-being, use my passion and true strengths, or leave me with enough energy to build Yes& at the capacity I craved. In time, I empowered myself to return to what I was called to pursue: full-time coaching. (You may remember my resignation phone call from chapter five.)

Get ready to cheer, "Begin again!"—because the next day, I applied for a full-time job.

WHAT!? Why? In hindsight, I can see this decision was made because I allowed my fears to drive the bus: "I cannot afford *not* to have a real job." The same storyline repeated itself because my underlying, limiting belief remained. Until I honestly illuminated and intentionally upheld or bravely challenged my money story, my actions and outcomes remained unchanged—even when I knew I wanted to change the actions and outcomes themselves.

Thus, I applied for and accepted a full-time job. Once again, I told myself it was a good idea. Once again, I faced my gut intuition that said it wasn't in alignment a few weeks in. I knew my talents, skills, and hungry passion were not being used to their fullest potential; I knew I was not experiencing the full potential of my life.

Although it felt scary, I refused to settle for a good-enough life when, in my gut, I knew the life I could create through full-time coaching would be marvelous. (Remember the quit list activity from chapter two? You're currently reading the details of my own.) I once again empowered myself to leave misalignment and pursue something better.

Thankfully, this time around, I began again with intentionality—rather than reaction. I challenge the underlying belief that promoted my cyclical, undesired actions and outcomes.

What's radical is the proof that follows. Three months after adopting a new-factory money belief, and acting in alignment with this belief, I experienced a life of abundance. I had not gone into debt as old me was terrified I would, I was not living paycheck to paycheck, I had not used my three-month emergency fund… In fact, embodying my new belief felt expansive.

This is not to say I have it all figured out. Nor is this to say my cyclical storyline or my old belief was bad. Each Alignment Journey cycle helped me develop greater awareness of myself, my values, and my needs; foster my ability to believe with intention; and take action toward my authentic, aligned life one baby-step action at a time.

There's a difference between spinning in circles and growing in a spiral. If you spin in circles, you will arrive at the same place or challenge without new awareness and insight.

If you grow in a spiral, you will recognize a pattern and use what you learn to begin again with a different approach.

Spinning in circles feels dizzying. Growing in a spiral feels familiar, but different, with each turn. Spinning in circles feels pointless. Growing in a spiral feels centered with a clear purpose that motivates you to persist.

To Begin Again Is Also to End Again

It is not uncommon for clients to sign a second or third contract with me after our initial six months together; most of my clients work with me for at least a year. I often witness tremendous growth in the first six months together related to the first three stages of the Alignment Journey: space, clarity, and direction. Then, when we arrive at the six-month mark, my clients often say something along the lines of: "I'm not done with you yet!!"

Once my clients have found and fostered their alignment toolbelt, they're ready to build something miraculous. So we do! We use heightened awareness, fresh perspectives, and the spiral growth journey to set new milestones and goals. They've already built the courage to take aligned, bold action. I proudly support my clients as they play and enjoy an upleveled version of the outdated life they had traversed for years.

Ultimately, however, there comes a time when our coaching relationship naturally concludes; my clients are confident with their tools, awareness, success stories, and authenticity to continue alone—or to face a different challenge or goal with a different support system.

When this moment arises, I beam with pride and admiration for the multiple Alignment Journeys we navigated together. I, too, trust their ability to begin again with something new. Nonetheless, it always feels a little sad—for both my clients and me—to let go of what was, to end something we cherished, to begin again, and to step away from coaching with Yes& and step into their next adventure.

You and I are nearly there, as well. Within the context of this book, as well as any other begin-again moment in your life, embrace all emotions that flow during this final stage of the Alignment Journey.

Begin Again Practice Four: When to Let Go

First, determine whether your cyclical pattern is one of spinning in circles or growing in a spiral. Does your recognized cycle lack new insights and feel dizzying or pointless? If so, you may be spinning in a circle. Make up your resolution, invite a trusted support system to point out your blind spot, or shift into something new to begin again with growth.

Does your recognized cycle include new insights, strengthen your self-awareness, and feel purposeful? If so, you're likely growing in an upward spiral! Continue to use your alignment tool belt, remain compassionate with your journey, and celebrate each new perspective or small shift as progress toward greater alignment.

In either instance, consider whether it may be time to leave the spiral or uplevel in a new way. Celebrate the growth you've already achieved, feel all the feelings associated with beginning and ending again, take a deep breath, and then go.

I believe in you. *You* can do this.

Gain access to additional Alignment Journey practices by downloading your Alignment Journey workbook at yesandbymarin.com/workbook.

CHAPTER 10

Ready Enough: You Are Not Alone

At some point, it is time to step forward confidently with your head held high. Your heart will race, and you will not be fully prepared. You're likely at least slightly naïve to the true magnitude of what is to come.

How beautiful: to be ready enough.

During my life coach training in Costa Rica, someone captured a photo of me on the beach as I stepped into the deep, mighty ocean. In the image, I hold a surfboard under my right arm, my shoulders are rolled back, and my eyes look to the distant horizon.

This image reminds me of *you,* regardless of whether you've surfed before or ever intend to, because it represents confidence in the wake of turbulence and challenge. It represents what it means to make a clear decision and take action, even in the face of uncertainty.

Furthermore, it reminds me of what came before this image: Pause on the shoreline. Overwhelm and intimidation in the face of a new journey. And this makes me even more proud of you for showing up to your ocean.

When I reflect on this image in relation to your Alignment Journey, I become even more passionate to ensure you continue your journey after you set this book down. Because your alignment matters, *you* matter, and although the shoreline may be more comfortable, I know you don't want to turn back, either.

Ironically, it's common to seek support as you prepare to enter the ocean, but not once you dare to step in. Yet it's when you're in the midst of experience, not prior to it, that you often need reminders to breathe, use your toolkit, and lean on the skills you developed.

Thus, allow me and everything within the Alignment Journey to guide and support you, not only leading up to change but in the midst of change, as you walk into your ocean.

You are fully prepared for whatever you are about to, or have already, walked into. *Please* do not turn your back on what you just realized. Foster your voice, build the support you need, and let's be darn sure you follow through.

You Have Permission

Historically, when I needed a boost in courage to continue my Alignment Journey, I reread an article titled "You Have Permission."

Recently, I clicked the article link saved in my bookmarks to discover it had been taken down. What an excellent opportunity to practice trust, to take a breath, remind myself that I already know, and share a message with you that has already stained my heart with compassion and determination.

The following poem is my interpretation of Tash Mitch's original article "You Have Permission." Before continuing onto whatever journey awaits you next, I invite you to take a breath, pause your worries and unending questions about *how*, and consider your answer is already in front of you.

You have permission to follow what you already know to be true; you have permission to live your full, authentic life.

> // You have permission //
> You have permission to dream wild dreams, to tune into that fiery passion that burns in your chest... and run with it in full trust.
>
> You have permission to be scared, to feel overwhelmed, or worried, or intimidated, or uncertain.
>
> You have permission to be absolutely confident in yourself, in your decisions, and skills, and current direction.
>
> You have permission to admit fault, to unapologetically ask for support, to reference your teachers, to reply "I don't know."

You have permission to love out loud; you have permission to dance on the street, to sing a cheerful hello to the Target cashier, to smile without reason—simply because that is your current expression.

You have permission to change your mind, to follow what feels right today, even if it differs from that which you predicted last week, or last year, or when you planned your life at age fifteen.

You have permission to pause. You have permission to rest. You are enough, already, regardless.

You have permission to work really hard on something not everyone may see as important, or logical, because you are passionate, and alive, and you know what feels crucial to your life expression.

You have permission to begin again and again and again and again and again.

You have permission to let good enough be good enough, to stay a while, to realize your current is not your ultimate, to be content rather than chase someone else's dream.

You have permission to demand your value, to take up space, to know your worth, and to let go of those who do not.

You have permission to mourn over a forgotten dream, or a plan that no longer suits you, over the outcome from a decision you made or your current experience if it is not what you hoped it to be.

You have permission to feel sad.

You have permission to go sledding alone at thirty-four, to pick up ice skating at age fifty, to change careers two months into the beginning of your first.

You have permission to do what you love, to be someone you love, to pursue a life you truly, deeply love.

You have permission to savor every minute… or wish some moments away.

You have permission to be absolutely content with your current life, just as it is. You also have permission to pursue another.

If you were waiting for someone to tell you these words, if you were waiting for a sign or a milestone, for another dollar or another year passed… Maybe, just maybe, this is it.

Align, and fully experience your authentic life.
Right now, or tomorrow, or next year.
You have permission.

I Am Here for You, and I Am Always Here for You

Even once my clients conclude working with me, I forever remain a part of their lives because I am the only one who experienced their Alignment Journey with them in full. Days, months, and years after working with clients, I am elated to receive messages about goals received, stories revisited, and new insights gained.

One of my clients laughed about her attempt at explaining our coaching sessions to her friends and family; no matter how many times or various ways she tried to do so, she could never quite articulate how impactful the visualizations, metaphors, and coaching experiences were for her. (You, too, now understand an inkling of what happens inside one-on-one coaching: shiny blue factories and Punky Brewster are only the beginning.)

Although I know very little, if anything, about you, I feel the same connection with you as I do my clients. You have read the intimacies of my life, my client stories, and learned of the Alignment Journey. For this reason, we will also forever be connected—and I am forever here to support you.

Individuals just like you are navigating their Alignment Journeys with excitement, courage, and wide eyes inside my membership program. We would love to officially welcome you into the Yes& community. Visit yesandbymarin.com/experience to learn more.

Read the Appendix for support practices and more information about coaching with Yes&.

Acknowledgements

Thank you to my coaches: Coby Kozlowski, Kristen Garaffo, Lindsay Gurley, Peter Will Benjamin, Kim Argetsinger, Michelle Knight, Cara Viana, Rachel Redmond, and every coach I will gratefully enlist for support as I continue on my journey.

Thank you to my one-on-one clients, who have believed in me since day one. Thank you to especially those who generously agreed to share their stories within this book.

Thank you to every member of the Yes& Experience, who continue to share their dreams, goals, and insights with me and the Yes& community. Thank you for your trust, vulnerability, and courage; I will forever feel proud and inspired with you.

Thank you to everyone who collaborated with me to make this book a reality: to author coach Jennifer Locke, editors Amy Calvin and Melinda Campbell, my cover and formatting design teams, and everyone at Self-Publishing School.

Thank you to the gorgeous individuals I am honored to call my friends: Boating School, Moontower, and the Morrison crew. Your fulfilling, supportive, and laughter-filled friendships keep me grounded amid big, bold dreams.

Thank you to Tyler Hitzeman, who has been by my side since Yes& was just a color scheme and who celebrated *Ready Enough* with me every step of the way.

With deep gratitude, thank you to the best family in the world: Mom, Dad, Colin, and Anastasia. To love and be loved by you is my most valued gift. I would be nowhere without you.

Lastly, thank you to *you*, who read these words. You are my why. Even if I do not yet know you, my belief in you and your dreams is beyond measure. Thank you for daring to explore, discover, and say yes to who you really are.

APPENDIX
Should I Hire a Life Coach?

For six years, I focused on the research behind the work I do today as a practitioner. I earned my bachelor's degree in general psychology and a master's degree in positive developmental psychology. I also received my life coaching and yoga certifications and attended personal development workshops at locations such as Kripalu Center for Yoga & Health in Massachusetts and Costa Rica Yoga Spa in Nosara.

I pride myself in combining creativity and flow with practices grounded in research—and I've come to learn, most new clients don't care about any of my certificates or diplomas. Instead of asking, "What certifications does this person have?," most clients start with "Is this investment worth it? Will this person help me?"

What makes answering this question tricky for coaching as a whole is how broad the industry has become. Coaching is currently an unregulated field. This means there are no required certifications, licensures, official boards, or direct degrees necessary for a practitioner to use the term "life coach." In fact, the title itself varies among coaches: "professional coach," "executive coach," and "health coach" are among the many nomenclatures in the field.

There is, however, a strong research base that provides evidence, evaluation, and guidance for the coaching industry via positive psychology: the scientific study of well-being and flourishing—defining a "good life" and how to get there. But even if your coach studied the field, that doesn't answer your question: Is coaching worth it? Can I trust this person?

For me, this comes down to clear communication and boundaries. To start, it is essential for practicing coaches to differentiate coaching from other forms of support. Coaching is not consulting, mentoring, therapy, or counseling—and should never be advertised as such. To me, it is a sign of a good coach if she or he refers clients to other means of support when necessary.

Unlike other helping fields, coaching fosters a learning process in which the client is the co-facilitator of her or his learning and growth. In contrast to consulting or advising, wherein the support system is seen as the expert, coaching considers the *client* as the expert and the coach as the expert guide.

A good coach facilitates their client in unveiling their own wisdom, values, and beliefs while working through client-centered goals, action steps, and roadblocks—and they do so through positive, solution-focused questions and observation. Therein, a coach must be creative and open to broad possibility to expand client perspectives rather than hinder them.

With coaching, you're not just going to go into another program where someone tells you what to do. YOU tell you what to do. For example, one of my clients expressed her pre coaching self as someone in "self-development burnout." She had read the books, pursued therapy to understand why and from where her roadblocks originated, knew what was wrong, but felt stuck about what to do next.

Similarly, another client expressed hesitation to enlist another support system because every solution in his past had failed. Once we dug into why, I heard his disappointment in every solution's emphasis on a cookie-cutter strategy rather than working through what he, individually, needed and desired. Furthermore, they failed to consider his preferences, reasoning, fears, and goals while creating a plan for his desired growth.

Coaching is different because it is intentionally not a one-size-fits-all style. Furthermore, coaches enter the room with curiosity rather than an assumption they already have the answer. This is because you know yourself best; it is a coach's job to help you hear your own voice, desires, fears, and deep-seated stories rather than blast you with more external noise and opinions.

You may question why you would enlist support in the first place if, ultimately, you have all of the answers you seek. Great question. In my experience, it is to expedite the self-discovery and alignment process. We all have blind spots we cannot see on our own: limiting beliefs, old storylines, and perspectives that we may think of as fact when it's truly one version of reality. By providing a space to question our own assumptions and unveil our beliefs, values, and desires, coaching collapses time.

Furthermore, we are social creatures. Going through your Alignment Journey alongside someone else is a heck of a lot more fun than doing it alone. Your dream is worth it, it is okay to feel afraid and ask for help, and it is freaking fun to celebrate together.

One of my favorite analogies to define coaching, shared throughout this book, is as follows: an Olympian seeks the support of a trainer not because they are incapable of training but because they aspire to be the absolute best. This can be you, too, if you choose.

In summary, a coach is likely worth your money and trust if they're adequately trained and clearly understand their qualification limitations—referring clients to other professional support systems when needed. Good coaches ask powerful, solution-focused questions while maintaining an environment of positivity and progression. Good coaches have traits such as respect, creativity, observation and neutrality. Lastly, a good coach practices self-reflection for consistent growth to provide themselves and their clients with continued, exceptional support.

The greatest test of all, however, is how you feel when you speak to a potential coach. What qualifies a good coach for you, and with regard to this particular season of your life?

Support Practice One: What Type of Support Works for You?

Start by asking yourself how you would define a good coach. What qualities, qualifications, approaches, and outcomes would make you feel supported? Create a job posting based on your own preferences, desires, and goals.

From here, consider what type of support systems are beneficial for you. Do you thrive in group environments? Do you enjoy an environment of like-minded peers, such as a mastermind—or do you prefer environments that have a clear leader? What types of support have you enjoyed in the past? Considering yourself in this moment, what type of support systems would be suitable to reach your current goals, work through your current challenges, and create a safe space to foster your best life?

Reasons to Work With a Coach

Reason One: You Desire More

A potential client, I'll refer to her as Kendra, told me during her coaching consultation that she was already pretty happy. She felt great about her current situation and, in fact, shared a lot of gratitude and positivity about where she was right now. But she anticipated change on the horizon—which induced feelings of anxiety. The one thing she knew upon entering our first call was what she did *not* want to do—but that didn't provide her with much clarity regarding what she wanted.

In just forty-five minutes of a coaching consultation, we created space and fostered clarity to understand why Kendra felt overwhelmed and unclear: her current reality already embodied what she desired.

Previously, she had dismissed this insight because she assumed her next step would be *different* than her current reality. It turns out, her mountain direction was to create more of what currently existed, with a few minor tweaks to spiral upward.

Now, Kendra had the foundation to ask better questions: rather than feeling overwhelmed with "What do I want moving forward?," she confidently asked, "What do I like about right now, and what few things are missing?" From there, she used her insights to feel excited, rather than lost, about what comes next.

A second example of enlisting the support of coaching to create a better life, even if your current life is pretty great, is my client Julianne (name changed for privacy). Julianne was my very first branding photographer for Yes&, and during our first shoot together, she prompted me to coach her in order to capture my work in action.

I distinctly remember the moment she paused her work, put down her camera, and said, "Wow, maybe I need to hire you as my coach."

Julianne wasn't seeking out coaching at the time of our meeting because she didn't know she needed a coach. In her case, and in the case of so many others, nothing in her life felt uncontrollably off course: her career wasn't horrible, her relationships weren't extremely unfulfilling, and she wasn't dissatisfied with her life. Rather, something felt *slightly* off—and typically, something feeling slightly off isn't a very strong catalyst to make a change (especially when compared to something like losing a job or wanting to pursue a lifelong dream).

After presenting the benefits of coaching, she took the leap to enlist my support. I'm honored to share that we've worked together for over two years and counting. Through coaching, she built unshakable self-confidence and self-trust—so much so that she's now courageously stepping into her own passionate entrepreneurial pursuit.

Not only did Julianne unveil what, precisely, felt off about her previously good life, she created space to clarify, direct, and act in alignment with big dreams moving forward, while maintaining the support of coaching to navigate her journey along the way.

Reason Two: You Need a Cheerleader

In opposition to not knowing exactly what's off, you may feel crystal clear about what you'd like to change in your life. A second reason many clients choose to enlist the support of a coach is to help them answer the question and work through the fear of *how*: "How the heck am I going to accomplish my goal?" "What if I fail?"

A beautiful example for this type of coaching support includes a client whom I'll refer to as Shayleigh. Shayleigh spent months searching for a new career path after being let go from her previous position. Although shocking, she expressed gratitude in her change in circumstance because it gave her an opportunity to step toward what she truly desired: professional organizing.

By the time of our introduction, Shayleigh had already made great progress to foster her courage and beliefs that working as a professional organizer was possible. Yet she struggled with *how* and what to do first.

The time, financial, and emotional investment of coaching felt scary, so she took a few days to create space for her feelings, desire, and intuition to settle. Shayleigh called me via video chat one week later to say yes; thus, her gorgeous and windy Alignment Journey officially began.

Throughout the next six months, we would experience many highs and lows together as she experimented with what pathway felt best for her. She applied for already established professional organizing companies and bravely explored the option to begin her own. She navigated seasons of doubt and momentarily entertained the idea of giving up—but she never did because part of her *how* included the accountability, dedicated space, and support of a one-on-one coach.

In absolute perfect timing, our twelfth and final session together concluded with her announcement that she landed an interview at her dream job. A few weeks later, I would receive a message of delight: her dream job, complete with her ideal start date and hours, had become a reality.

Reason Three: You Need a Kick in the Butt

A third common reason clients of mine have chosen to enlist the support of a coach is because they needed a kick in the ass. This reason includes you if you want someone to *never* permit you to let go or lose sight of your dream—to ensure you will not fall back on limiting beliefs, old storylines, or familiar, self-sabotaging patterns that otherwise repeat over and over and over again.

As your coach, that's exactly what I'm here for; I am here to ensure your dream survives through all stages of the Alignment Journey—from space to clarity, direction to action, riding the waves to celebration, and beginning again.

During a recent coaching consultation, a client shared this: "I always let someone else's dreams take precedence over my own. Frankly," he added, "I'm sick of it." He went on to proclaim why this time would be different, and we set up a plan to ensure he remained in alignment.

This client, whom I'll refer to as Mateo, felt absolutely burnt out from corporate life and was eager to begin his next chapter—but he felt just comfortable enough in his current role to remain. Mateo was aware of comfort's double-edged sword I hear many clients speak to: he was comfortable *enough* to convince himself to stay in a fine life even though he wasn't satisfied or fulfilled—and even though the lifestyle was depleting his mental and physical health.

Until we started working together, Mateo entertained a cycle of "comfortable enough" to remain in misalignment for just another day—which turned into just another week, just another month, and just another year… Recall the benefit of discomfort in the oh sh!t stage of your Alignment Journey—sometimes, we need to stand up from our lawn chair so we can experience, rather than observe, our mountain.

As you've read about throughout this book, I, too, have taken big scary leaps toward big scary goals. Because of this, I challenge my clients to pursue greater alignment *while* holding compassion and empathy for the fear bound to arise when we leave comfortable, safe alternatives. But no matter how long it takes, or how many layers we must create space to explore, I always ensure you move toward your dream—because it is always worth it; alignment is worth it.

So what happened to the corporate client? After three weeks of working together, Mateo was presented a perfect opportunity to leave his job on good terms—and he said yes! His confidence, pride, and obvious relief was stunning.

Reason Four: You Refuse to Settle for Less

This reason to enlist support requires a perspective shift from what society historically considered essential for well-being and health because something isn't necessarily wrong or mis-aligned in this scenario. With no problem to solve, you may question why you would spend valuable resources to change: "Why would I spend this much money if life is fine?"

The answer lies in your ability to taste what else is possible for your life—and to deem it a worthy pursuit. The individuals who hire me for this reason dream of lives bigger than good enough: "I want to experience more purpose and meaning." "I want to make a greater impact." "I want to dream bigger or do bigger or create something *bigger.*"

To clarify, sometimes good enough *is* good enough— and I'm all for contentment. But if there's something on your heart, something calling you—a twinkle in your eye or something on the horizon that feels exciting to pursue— there's a reason, and you deserve to go after it.

You deserve to live a life that feels incredible, that feels beyond your wildest dreams, that feels as if you are experiencing the full breath this life has to offer you. Please follow your call and allow your life to shine bright and shine bold. Remember, living brightly will not only benefit you, it will inspire others to live a life beyond their wildest dreams as well.

While writing this book, one of my clients was building a math tutoring business. Throughout our time together, he consistently repeated in shock and awe that he had created his dream career. Our work together allowed him to hold space for his ideal, foster belief (through the entire ride) his ideal was possible, and celebrate where his ideal already existed.

Coaching was his space for encouragement to continue forward—even when curveballs were thrown his way, even when it felt scary, even when finances felt tight, and the *how* didn't feel crystal clear. It was all okay because in the midst of everything, he still woke up every day and knew, for certain, this was the life he chose to live; this was his greatest alignment.

Support Practice Two: Consider Support

Do you relate with any of my client stories? Do you desire support to improve your life in some capacity, cheer on your dreams, gain accountability for your goals, or stay accountable to your true ideals?

If so, dare to inquire. Visit yesandbymarin.com or find another coach who excites your current needs and desires.

Addressing Common Roadblocks

Two excuses I hear from individuals hesitant to enlist support on their Alignment Journey are I don't have enough time and I don't have enough money.

When I was a senior in high school, I started voice lessons only to quit a few weeks in. "I don't have enough time," I'd told my instructor. To this, my instructor looked me dead in the eye and said, without apology, "No, you're not *making* time."

Initially, I was offended and defensive. "No way! I dance twenty hours a week, I'm in two AP classes, I have hours of homework plus university applications to complete…!" In hindsight, I look back on this moment and realize she was right. I had enough time, and although I could deliver a similar list of excuses today, I truly believe there is *always* enough time.

In summary, it is often not about time. It is about what we choose to value and prioritize. The same goes for money.

Do you not have enough money to buy a new car? Or do you prioritize weekend hangouts that equate to the cost of a vehicle down payment over the course of one year?

Do you truly not have enough time to make breakfast? Or did you prioritize Instagram for thirty minutes after your alarm went off?

Do you not have time to call your parents? Or is your value of family connection fulfilled with one monthly call rather than someone else's weekly expectation?

Importantly, none of the above are bad or wrong (nor are they good or right)—they just are. I didn't value voice lessons in high school enough to sacrifice my time in the dance studio. Six years later, I spent money I "didn't have" and time that "didn't exist" to sing my heart out every week during grad school.

Sometimes, it *is* a means of saving up, delegating, or working through a season of life when resources are sparse. I do not intend to negate the reality of difficult circumstances nor assume your own. Rather, I empower you to see where opportunity *does* exist in your life to practice autonomy and abundance—especially if you feel called to take action toward a life of greater alignment.

Support Practice Three: Resource Alignment

Make three columns on a page. In the first column, make a list that outlines your greatest values and goals. In the second column, write out your greatest expenses. In the third column, write out your greatest time and energy expenditures.

When you compare these three lists, do they match? In other words, would someone conclude your values from column one after reading your bank statement or viewing your calendar?

Support Practice Four: Look in Your Resource Mirror

Try this experiment: Look in the mirror and ask yourself, "Am I willing to invest in my best life? Do I trust the return will far surpass the current risk?"

Further, consider when you have invested in yourself before with time or money. When have you taken a risk in full trust and belief that your return on investment was definite? Where are you hesitant to invest in your most full, authentic life—and what would it take to convince your inner fears and gremlins to believe your intuition?

Learn how you can begin your Alignment Journey with Marin's life-changing coaching support at yesandbymarin.com/experience.

YOUR GOLDEN TICKET

Congratulations for completing *Ready Enough*!

In celebration of your vulnerable and courageous exploration, I'm gifting you a golden ticket to join my group membership program. There are no long-term commitments, and you can use your discount with any of your three membership options.

Begin your next journey at
yesandbymarin.com/experience

Receive $50 off your first month as a
Yes& Experience member!

Use coupon code "AlignmentJourney"
at checkout.

ABOUT THE AUTHOR

As a coach, author, and speaker, Marin Laukka empowers you to break free from false expectations and limiting beliefs about what *should* be so you can own your potential, unapologetically make your positive impact, and experience true fulfillment.

Marin holds a master's degree in positive psychology and certifications in life coaching and yoga. Her approach balances the importance of research-based practice with authentic life experience to guide clients toward true fulfillment. She is proud to share client testimonials that describe her support as "unparalleled" and "truly the most influential decision I've made for my health and well-being."

Writing a book has been a dream of Marin's since first grade. She is overjoyed to release *Ready Enough* as her first book, with an instinct there are many more to come.

To learn more about Marin, read her full story at yesandbymarin.com.

A Note From the Author's Dog

Hi! My name is Aatto, and my mom is the author of this book. I think I should be a co-author because I slept at her feet whenever she wrote and reminded her to take a break for our daily walks.

Did you enjoy our book!? We would be grateful if you left an honest review on Amazon to share your experience. Scanning the QR code below with your phone camera will send you directly where you need to go.

Thank you for helping us get this book into the hands of those who need it most. Your review is greatly appreciated!

Made in United States
North Haven, CT
28 November 2021